Many Religions—One Covenant

JOSEPH CARDINAL RATZINGER

Many Religions— One Covenant

Israel, the Church, and the World

TRANSLATED BY GRAHAM HARRISON

WITH A FOREWORD
BY SCOTT HAHN

IGNATIUS PRESS   SAN FRANCISCO

Title of the German original:
Die Vielfalt der Religionen
und der Eine Bund
© 1998 Verlag Urfeld GmbH, Hagen

Cover photograph:
Dome of the Rock and Western Wall
CORBIS/David H. Wells

Cover design by Roxanne Mei Lum

CONTENTS

II. THE NEW COVENANT

On the Theology of the Covenant in the New Testament

III. THE NEW MANNA

Homily for the 19th Sunday in Year B, 1997

IV. THE DIALOGUE OF THE RELIGIONS AND THE RELATIONSHIP BETWEEN JUDAISM AND CHRISTIANITY

FOREWORD

by Scott Hahn

This book is a majestic bridge, fashioned by a master builder.

In *Many Religions—One Covenant*, Cardinal Joseph Ratzinger spans the deep divides in modern Catholic scholarship to present a compelling study in biblical theology, modern in its concerns yet classical in its breadth. It is his classical mastery, his *ressourcement*, that enables the Cardinal to build a bridge.

There can be no doubt that contemporary theology needs a bridge. Following the trend in secular academia, theology has fragmented into many isolated disciplines, each working in isolation from all the others—the condition Jacques Barzun describes as "specialism". Thus, dogmatic theologians often assume they have nothing to learn from biblical scholars. Exegetes, for their part, give scant consideration to the insights of systematic and dogmatic theologians. To many scholars, these disciplines are almost contradictory: doctrine is the "opposite" of Scripture.

Yet, amid the many varieties of theological experience, the author of this volume sees a profound unity. His synthesis will, perhaps, strike readers as novel; but it is actually a recovery of the great Catholic tradition, not only of the Scholastics and the Fathers, but of the Apostles themselves.

For, though the divisions are deep, they are not very old. They reach back, rather, to the aftermath of the Protestant Reformation. Whenever heresies arise, the Church must treat dogma in a way that does not give due proportion to the whole truth. Instead, theologians must emphasize precisely the points that heretics deny. For example, because the Protestant reformers emphasized faith sometimes at the expense of works, post-Reformation Catholic theology has tended to emphasize works more than faith. Because Protestants preached ''Scripture alone'' apart from tradition, Catholics have had to emphasize sacred tradition to a greater degree than before.

All this was necessary, in a remedial way. Yet its lingering effect has been to produce a theology that majors in relatively minor points. After all, tradition itself teaches the primacy of Scripture, and Catholic authorities from Saint Paul onward have taught the priority of faith over works. In classical theology, faith and works, Scripture and tradition, all receive their due, because all belong to one essential reality, whose archetypal expression is in the Word of God.

Thus, the revealed Word is, as it were, the support for every length of the Cardinal's theological bridge. Indeed, the Bible is the model he chooses for his theology, a fact he has acknowledged in his *Principles of Catholic Theology*: ''The writers of Holy Scripture speak as themselves, as men, and yet, precisely in doing so, they are *theo-logoi*, those through whom God as subject, as the word that speaks itself, enters history. . . . [Thus] the Bible becomes the model of all theology."

Yet, more than a mere blueprint, the Bible is theology's singular authority. Later in the same work, Cardinal Ratzinger adds: "*The normative theologians* are the authors of Holy Scripture" (emphasis mine). And finally he addresses the Bible as the fulfillment of theology: "Scripture alone is theology in the fullest sense of the word, because it truly has God as its subject; it does not just speak of him but *is* his own speech."

Neither does he make apologies, as a dogmatic theologian, for such an overwhelming biblical emphasis. Like his patristic and scholastic ancestors, he transcends academic overspecialization. Far from being opposites, doctrine and Scripture are irreducibly united in Cardinal Ratzinger's work. He has gone so far as to say that "dogma is by definition nothing other than an interpretation of Scripture". His insight has been confirmed by the most august group of his fellow theologians, the International Theological Commission, in its 1989 document *On the Interpretation of Dogmas*: "In the dogma of the Church, one is thus concerned with the correct interpretation of the Scriptures." Dogma, then, is the Church's infallible exegesis, and dogmatic theology is a reflection upon that work.

What happens, then, when a theologian such as Joseph Ratzinger, following from the principles outlined above, seeks to deepen our understanding of the Bible's most fundamental principle? The answer is on every page of this book. For the covenant *defines* religion for Christians and Jews. We cannot discern God's design or his will if we do not meditate upon his covenant. As far back as the second century, Saint Irenaeus wrote: "Understanding . . . consists in showing why there are a number of covenants with mankind and in teaching what is the character of those covenants."

The covenant, then, is the principle that unites the New Testament with the Old, the Scriptures with tradition, and each of the various branches of theology with all the others. The covenant does more than bridge the gaps between these elements; it fills in the gaps, so that biblical scholarship, dogmatic theology, and magisterial authority all stand on common ground—solid ground. All are firmly grounded in Jesus Christ. In the words of the International Theological Commission: "The theological interpretation of Scripture should start with Jesus Christ as the center of Scripture."

Thus, Cardinal Ratzinger demonstrates that theologians and exegetes need one another. For theology is dependent upon the correct interpretation of Scripture. And exegesis, for its part, depends upon theology. Exegetes, after all, are not like botanists examining the leaves of a tree. They are men who are trying to examine Paul's motives and think Peter's thoughts, and John's—and God's! Exegesis, properly pursued, *is* theology. Again, quoting Cardinal Ratzinger: "Being itself a theological discipline, . . . exegesis has close and complex relationships with other fields of theological learning."

Though defensive theology is necessary in times of heresy, it is hardly an ideal for times of peace. In this book, as in all his books, Cardinal Ratzinger provides a model for true *ressourcement*—not just a recovery of the Fathers, but a return to the place where the Fathers returned, again and again: the living oracles, the Word of God.

With the recovery of the covenant comes a recovery of what the British Benedictine Anscar Vonier called "true classicism in Christianity". By renewing the Church's appreciation of the new covenant, Cardinal Ratzinger proposes a fully integrated Christian life, with Christ at the center of the Scriptures, but also at the center of the Church today. For in the Eucharist he is still, as ever, fulfilling the old covenant and ratifying the new.

Many Religions—One Covenant is a book we theologians, and other believing Catholics, have long awaited. Let us cross that bridge, now that we have come to it.

PREFACE

The historical upheaval of 1989 also brought about a change of topic in theology. Liberation theology, understood in political terms, had given a new, political shape to questions about redemption and about the world's hope, questions that had long been pushed to one side. In doing so, however, it had presented politics with a task it could not fulfill. Of course, the basic themes of liberation theology—the search for peace, justice, and the protection of creation—are still current, but now they are conceived in more modest terms and within a different framework. This different framework is, above all, the dialogue with the world religions, a dialogue that has become increasingly necessary in a world where cultures are more and more encountering and interpenetrating one another. In the last chapter of this little book I give at least some brief indications of the pitfalls and hopes involved in such a dialogue.

The other topic that has come to the fore in theology is the question of the relationship between the Church and Israel. One of the things contributing to the new urgency of this question—although it is definitely neither the only reason for it nor the only way of assessing it—is the awareness of a long-repressed guilt, which has branded the Christian conscience in the wake of the terrible events of the twelve lamentable years from 1933 to 1945. The historico-critical method makes Christian interpretation of the Old Testament seem largely dubious; New Testament exegesis has increasingly relativized Christology. Initially these two factors seem to favor dialogue between Christians and Jews: now (it might appear) the Jewish interpretation of the Old Testament is the only one that can be regarded as historically justified. And by dismantling much of Christology, it should be possible to remove the stumbling stone that separates Jewish faith from Christianity.

Such prognostications are deceptive, however. For if the Old Testament does not speak of Christ, it is not a Bible for Christians. Long ago Harnack had already drawn the conclusion that it was high time to follow Marcion and separate Christianity from the Old Testament. However, this would dissolve Christian identity, which is founded on the unity of the Testaments. At the same time it would dissolve the inner relationship that links us to Israel and result in those very consequences which Marcion had formulated: the God of Israel would appear as an alien God, definitely not the God of Christians.

The same thing would apply if we were to dismantle Christology. If Christ were only a misunderstood Jewish rabbi or a political rebel executed by the Romans for political reasons, what significance would his message have now? Through him whom the Church believes to be Jesus Christ and Son of God, the God of Israel has become the God of the nations, fulfilling the prophecy that the Servant of God would bring the light of this God to the nations. If the light of Christ goes out, God's light is also extinguished; for it is in the face of Christ that we have seen the light of God, the light of the one God in whom we believe, together with "Abraham and his seed". For the Christian conviction is that, through this faith, we are privileged to count ourselves children of Abraham. False simplifications only do damage to the dialogue with the religions and to the dialogue with the Jewish faith.

I first encountered the topic of the relationship between the two Testaments, and of their inner unity-in-diversity, in a course of lectures delivered by Gottlieb Söhngen in the Munich Faculty of Theology in the winter semester of 1947–48. The question has stayed with me ever since, but it was the new challenges of recent years that prompted me to take an active part in this dialogue, which theology is now pursuing with increasing interest. In my present situation it is impossible for me to develop systematic theological ideas; nonetheless, as I see more and more clearly in retrospect, the requests that reach me, asking me to participate in the dialogue, reflect the actual priorities of the ecclesiological and theological situation. The four chapters of this little book arose from just such concrete occasions. I need hardly say that they are no more than slight and tentative approaches to the great topic; however, fragmentary as they are, they can perhaps pro-

mote the questioning process. I myself would not have
had the temerity to put them together into a book; but
I did not want to reject the invitation to do so that
came to me from the Friends of the Integrated Community.[1] My hope is that this tiny opus, with all its
limitations, can help us to a better understanding of
the message that the *one* Bible addresses to us.

Rome, Advent 1997

JOSEPH CARDINAL RATZINGER

[1] The Catholic Integrated Community (Katholische Integrierte Gemeinde) has been established as a "public association" according to
canon 301 of the Code of Canon Law in the six dioceses of Munich
and Freising, Rottenburg-Stuttgart, Augsburg, Morogoro (Tanzania),
Rome, and Vienna. Its origins go back to the Catholic youth movement. It was more formally organized in 1968 in Munich. Its goal
is to be a new form of apostolic life with a *vita communis* of families
and celibates inspired by the Acts of the Apostles 2:42–47. Recently a
new emphasis has been the effort to foster a new encounter between
the Jewish people and the Church.

I

ISRAEL, THE CHURCH, AND THE WORLD

Their Relation and Mission, according to the 1992 *Catechism of the Catholic Church*

The history of the relationship between Israel and Christendom is drenched with blood and tears. It is a history of mistrust and hostility, but also—praise be to God—a history marked again and again by attempts at forgiveness, understanding, and mutual acceptance.

This essay was written for the great Jewish-Christian meeting that took place in Jerusalem in February 1994 under the expert and dynamic chairmanship of Rabbi Rosen. Initially I thought that this Congress was to be a theological dialogue between Christians and Jews, on the subject of their common inheritance, on the one hand, and what divided them, on the other. Consequently, I set forth what the Catechism has taught on this problem. Only later did I realize that the Congress was not actually concerned with the religious dialogue between Christians and Jews but was to discuss how religious leadership could take place in a secularized world. The representatives of the various communities were to speak of their own experience, and the issues raised were to be explored in depth in work-groups. Since, however, the question of the foundations of a common approach could not be entirely ignored, it seemed useful to go ahead

The mission of reconciliation

After Auschwitz the mission of reconciliation and acceptance permits no deferral. Even if we know that Auschwitz is the gruesome expression of an ideology that not only wanted to destroy Judaism but also hated and sought to eradicate from Christianity its Jewish heritage, the question remains: What could be the reason for so much historical hostility between those who actually must belong together because of their faith in the one God and commitment to his will?

Does this hostility result from something in the very faith of Christians? Is it something in the "essence of Christianity", so that one would have to prescind from Christianity's core, deny Christianity its heart, in order to come to real reconciliation?

---

with the address I had prepared. In order to relate my remarks to the overall theme of the Congress, I tried to conclude by briefly indicating the consequences of these perspectives for our shared responsibility in the secularized world. Since my address was written on the basis of the Bible and the Catechism, it did not seem necessary subsequently to add bibliographical references; they are not hard to find. [This talk was given in English.]

This contribution was first published in HEUTE—*pro ecclesia viva. Das Heft der Integrierten Gemeinde*, No. 1: *Vom Wieder-Einwurzeln im Jüdischen als einer Bedingung für das Einholen des Katholischen* (Bad Tölz, 1994; 2d ed., 1995), 152–69. Then it was republished in Joseph Cardinal Ratzinger, *Evangelium, Katechese, Katechismus: Streiflichter auf den Katechismus der Katholischen Kirche* (Munich: Verlag Neue Stadt, 1995), 63–83. (English trans.: *Gospel, Catechesis, Catechism: Sidelights on the Catechism of the Catholic Church* [San Francisco, 1997], 73–97.)

This is an assumption that some Christian thinkers have in fact made in the last few decades in reaction to the horrors of history. Do confession of Jesus of Nazareth as the Son of the living God and faith in the Cross as the redemption of mankind contain an implicit condemnation of the Jews as stubborn and blind, as guilty of the death of the Son of God? Could it be that the very core of the faith of Christians compels intolerance, even hostility toward the Jews? And, conversely, could the self-esteem of Jews and the defense of their historic dignity and deepest convictions oblige them to demand that Christians abandon the heart of their faith and so require Jews similarly to forsake tolerance? Is the conflict programmed in the heart of religion and only to be overcome through its repudiation?

Reconciliation without abandoning the Christian faith?

In this heightened framing of the question, the problem confronting us today reaches far beyond an academic interreligious dialogue into the fundamental decisions of this historic hour. One sees more frequent attempts to mollify the issue by representing Jesus as a Jewish teacher who in principle did not go beyond what was possible in Jewish tradition. His execution is understood to result from the political tensions between Jews and Romans. In point of fact, he was executed by the Roman authority in the way political rebels were punished. His elevation to Son of God is accordingly understood to have occurred after the fact, in a Hellenistic climate; at the same time, in view of the given political circumstances, the blame for the crucifixion is transferred from the Romans to the Jews. As a challenge to exegesis, such interpretations can further an acute listening to the text and perhaps produce something useful. However, they do not speak of the Jesus of the historical sources but instead construct a new and different Jesus, relegating the historical faith in the Christ of the Church to mythology. Christ appears as a product of Greek religiosity and political opportunism in the Roman Empire. One does not do justice to the gravity of the question with such a view; indeed, one retreats from it.

Thus the question remains: Can Christian faith, retaining its inner power and dignity, not only tolerate Judaism but accept it in its historic mission? Or can it not? Can there be true reconciliation without abandoning the faith, or is reconciliation tied to such abandonment?

The presentation in the *Catechism of the Catholic Church*

In reply to this question, which concerns us most deeply, I shall not present simply my own views. Rather I wish to show what the *Catechism of the Catholic Church*, released in 1992, has to say. This work has been published by the Magisterium of the Catholic Church as an authentic expression of her faith. In recognition of the significance of Auschwitz and from the mission of the Second Vatican Council, the matter of reconciliation has been inscribed in the Catechism as an object of faith. Let us see, then, how the Catechism stands in relation to our question in terms of its definition of its own mission.

1. Jews and Pagans in the Account of the Magi from the Orient (Mt 2:1–12)

I begin with the text of the Catechism explaining the significance of the account of the journey of the Magi from the East. It sees in the Magi the origin of the Church formed out of the pagans; the Magi afford an enduring reflection on the way of the pagans. The Catechism says the following:

> The magi's coming to Jerusalem in order to pay homage to the king of the Jews shows that they seek in Israel, in the messianic light of the star of David, the one who will be king of the nations. Their coming means that the pagans can discover Jesus and worship him as Son of God and Savior of the world only by turning toward the Jews and receiving from them the messianic promise as contained in the Old Testament. The Epiphany shows that the "full number of the nations" now takes its "place in the family of the patriarchs", and acquires *Israelitica dignitas* (are made "worthy of the heritage of Israel") (528).

Jesus' mission: To unite Jews and pagans

In this text, we can see how the Catechism views the relationship between Jews and the nations of the world as communicated by Jesus; in addition, it offers at the same time a first presentation of the mission of Jesus. Accordingly, we say that the mission of Jesus is to unite Jews and pagans into a single People of God in which the universalist promises of the Scriptures are fulfilled that speak again and again of the nations worshiping the God of Israel—to the point where in Trito-Isaiah we no longer read merely of the pilgrimage of the nations to Zion but of the proclamation of the mission of ambassadors to the nations "that have not heard my fame or seen my glory. . . . And some of them also I will take for priests and for Levites, says the Lord" (Is 66:19, 21).

In order to present this unification of Israel, and the nations, the brief text—still interpreting Matthew 2 —gives a lesson on the relationship of the world religions, the faith of Israel, and the mission of Jesus: the world religions can become the star that enlightens men's path, that leads them in search of the kingdom of God. The star of the religions points to Jerusalem, it is extinguished and lights up anew in the Word of God, in the Sacred Scripture of Israel. The Word of God preserved herein shows itself to be the true star without which or bypassing which the goal cannot be found.

When the Catechism designates the star as the "star of David", it links the account of the Magi, furthermore, with the Balaam prophecy of the star that shall come forth out of Jacob (Num 24:17), seeing this prophecy for its part connected to Jacob's blessing of Judah, which promised the ruler's staff and scepter to him who is owed "the obedience of the peoples" (Gen 49:10). The Catechism sees Jesus as the promised shoot of Judah, who unites Israel and the nations in the kingdom of God.

Abraham's history is to be the history of all

What does all this mean? The mission of Jesus consists in bringing together the histories of the nations in the community of the history of Abraham, the history of Israel. His mission is unification, reconciliation, as the Letter to the Ephesians (2:18–22) will then present it. The history of Israel should become the history of all, Abraham's sonship is to be extended to the "many". This course of events has two aspects to it: the nations can enter into the community of the promises of Israel in entering into the community of the one God, who now becomes and must become the way of all because there is only one God and because his will is therefore truth for all. Conversely, this means that all nations, without the abolishment of the special mission of Israel, become brothers and receivers of the promises of the Chosen People; they become People of

God with Israel through adherence to the will of God and through acceptance of the Davidic kingdom.

"Salvation is from the Jews"

Yet another observation can be important here. If the account of the Magi, as the Catechism interprets it, presents the answer of the sacred books of Israel as the decisive and indispensable guide for the nations, in doing so, it varies the same theme we encounter in John's Gospel in the formula: "Salvation is from the Jews" (4:22). This heritage remains abidingly vital and contemporary in the sense that there is no access to Jesus, and thereby there can be no entrance of the nations into the People of God, without the acceptance in faith of the revelation of God who speaks in the Sacred Scripture that Christians term the Old Testament.

By way of summary, we can say: Old and New Testaments, Jesus and the Sacred Scripture of Israel, appear here as indivisible. The new thrust of his mission to unify Israel and the nations corresponds to the prophetic thrust of the Old Testament itself. Reconciliation in the common recognition of the kingdom of God, recognition of his will as the way, is the nucleus of Jesus' mission, in which person and message are indivisible. This mission is efficacious already at the moment when he lies silent in the crib. One understands nothing about him if one does not enter with him into the dynamic of reconciliation.

2. Jesus and the Law: Not to Abolish but to "Fulfill"

Nevertheless the great vision of this text gives rise to a question. How will that which is foreshadowed here in the image of the star and those who follow it be historically realized? Does the historic image of Jesus, do his message and his work, correspond to this vision, or do they contradict it?

Now there is nothing more contested than the question of the historical Jesus. The Catechism as a book of faith proceeds from the conviction that the Jesus of the Gospels is also the only true historical Jesus. Starting here, it presents the message of Jesus first under the all-encompassing motto "Kingdom of God", in which the various aspects of the good news of Jesus coalesce, so that they receive from here their direction and their concrete content (541–60).

Then the Catechism goes on to show the relation Jesus-Israel from three vantage points: Jesus and the Law (577–82), Jesus and the Temple (583–86), Jesus and the faith of Israel in the one God and Savior (587–91). At this juncture our book comes finally to the decisive fate of Jesus, to his death and Resurrection, in which Christians see the Passover mystery of Israel fulfilled and brought to its final theological depth.

Jesus and Israel

The central chapter on Jesus and Israel interests us here
particularly. It is also fundamental for the interpretation
of the concept of kingdom of God and for the understanding of the Easter mystery. Now, to be sure, the
very themes of Law, Temple, and the oneness of God
are the volatile ones supplying the material for Jewish-
Christian disputes. Is it even possible to view these
things simultaneously in fidelity to history, according
to faith, and under the primacy of reconciliation?

It is not only earlier interpretations of the history of
Jesus that have given generally negative images to Pharisees, priests, and Jews. Indeed, crass contrasts have become a cliché in modern and liberal descriptions where
Pharisees and priests are portrayed as the representatives of a hardened legalism, as representatives of the
eternal law of the establishment presided over by religious and political authorities who hinder freedom and
live from the oppression of others. In light of these interpretations, one sides with Jesus, fights his fight, by
coming out against the power of priests in the Church
and against law and order in the State. The images of
the enemy in contemporary liberation struggles fuse
with those of Jesus' history, which is reduced to a
struggle against religiously veiled domination of man
by man, the inauguration of that revolution in which
Jesus is, to be sure, the underdog but precisely by his
defeat establishes a first step that will necessarily lead

to definitive victory. If Jesus is seen thus, if his death must be conceived in terms of this constellation of antitheses, his message cannot be one of reconciliation.

Jesus' fidelity to the Law

It goes without saying that the Catechism does not share this outlook. Rather it holds principally to the portrayal of Jesus in the Gospel of Matthew, seeing in Jesus the Messiah, the greatest in the kingdom of heaven; as such he knew he was "to fulfill the Law by keeping it in its all-embracing detail . . . down to 'the least of these commandments' " (578).

The Catechism thus connects the special mission of Jesus to his fidelity to the Law; it sees in him the servant of God who truly brings justice (Is 42:3) and thereby becomes "a covenant to the people" (Is 42:6; CCC 580). Our text is far removed here from any superficial smoothing-over of Jesus' conflict-laden history, however. Instead of interpreting his way superficially in the sense of an ostensibly prophetic attack on hardened legalism, it strives to fathom its real theological depth.

This is seen clearly in the following passage: the "principle of integral observance of the Law not only in letter but in spirit was dear to the Pharisees. By giving Israel this principle they had led many Jews of Jesus' time to an extreme religious zeal. This zeal, were it not to lapse into 'hypocritical' casuistry, could only prepare the People for the unprecedented intervention

of God through the perfect fulfillment of the Law by
the only Righteous One in place of all sinners" (579).
This perfect fulfillment includes Jesus taking upon himself the " 'curse of the Law' incurred by those who do
not 'abide by the things written in the book of the
Law, and do them' " (Gal 3:10, CCC 580). The death
on the Cross is thus theologically explained by its innermost solidarity with the Law and with Israel; the
Catechism in this regard presents a link to the Day of
Atonement and understands Christ's death itself as the
great event of atonement, as the perfect realization of
what the signs of the Day of Atonement signify (433;
578).

Fulfillment of the Torah
through the Law of the Gospel

With these statements we find ourselves at the center
of the Christian-Jewish dialogue, we reach the juncture
where we are faced with the decisive choice between
reconciliation and alienation.

Before we pursue further the interpretation of the
figure of Jesus as it emerges here, we must, however,
first ask what this view of the historical figure of Jesus
means for the existence of those who know themselves
to be grafted through him onto the "olive tree Israel",
the children of Abraham.

Where the conflict between Jesus and the Judaism
of his time is presented in a superficial, polemical way,
a concept of liberation is derived that can understand

the Torah only as a slavery to external rites and observances.

The view of the Catechism derived essentially from The Gospel of Matthew and finally from the entirety of the tradition of the Gospels leads logically to quite a different perception, which I would like to quote in detail:

> The Law of the Gospel *fulfills the commandments* of the Law [= the Torah]. The Lord's Sermon on the Mount, far from abolishing or devaluing the moral prescriptions of the Old Law, releases their hidden potential and has new demands arise from them: it reveals their entire divine and human truth. It does not add new external precepts, but proceeds to renew the heart, the root of human acts, where man chooses between the pure and impure, where faith, hope, and charity are found. . . . The Gospel thus brings the Law to its fullness through imitation of the perfection of the heavenly Father (1968).

The unity between the good news of Jesus and the message of Sinai

This view of a deep unity between the good news of Jesus and the message of Sinai is again summarized in the reference to a statement of the New Testament that is not only common to the Synoptic tradition but also has a central role in the Johannine and Pauline writings: the whole Law, including the Prophets, depends on the twofold yet one commandment of love of God and love of neighbor (CCC 1970; Mt 7:12; 22:34–40; Mk 12:38–43; Lk 10:25–28; Jn 13:34; Rom 13:8–10). For the nations, being assumed into the children of Abraham is concretely realized in entering into the will of God in which moral commandment and profession of the oneness of God are indivisible, as this becomes clear especially in Saint Mark's version of this tradition, in which the double commandment is expressly linked to the "Sh^{e}ma Israel", to the Yes to the one and only God. Man's way is prescribed for him; he is to measure himself according to the standard of God and according to his own human perfection.

At the same time, the ontological depth of these statements comes to the fore. By saying Yes to the double commandment, man lives up to the call of his nature to be the image of God that was willed by the Creator and is realized as such in loving with the love of God.

Beyond all historical and strictly theological discussions, we find ourselves placed at the heart of the question of the present responsibility of Jews and Christians before the modern world. This responsibility consists precisely in representing the truth of the one will of God before the world and thus placing man before his inner truth, which is at the same time his way. Jews and Christians must bear witness to the one God, to the Creator of heaven and earth, and do this in that entirety which Psalm 19 formulates in an exemplary way: the light of the physical creation, the sun, and the spiritual light, the commandment of God, belong inextricably together. In the radiance of the Word of God the same God speaks to the world who attests to himself in the sun, moon, and stars, in the beauty and fullness of creation. [In the words of the German hymn:] "Die Sonne ist des Himmels Ehr, doch dein Gesetz, Herr, noch viel mehr . . ." [The sun is heaven's pride, yet your law, Lord, much more besides].

3. Jesus' Interpretation of the Law: Conflict and Reconciliation

The inevitable question follows. Does such a view of the relationship between the Law and the Gospel not come down to an unacceptable attempt at harmonization? How does one explain, then, the conflict that led to Jesus' Cross? Does all of this not stand in contradiction to Saint Paul's interpretation of the figure of Jesus? Are we not denying here the entire Pauline doctrine of grace in favor of a new moralism, thereby abolishing the "articulus stantis et cadentis ecclesiae", the essential innovation of Christianity? With respect to this point, the section on morality in the Catechism, from which we took the discussion of the Christian way, corresponds closely to the depiction of Christ taken from the dogmatic section. If we attend carefully we see two essential aspects of the issue in which the answer to our questions lies.

The interrelation of both Testaments

In its presentation of the inner continuity and coherence of the Law and the Gospel, which we have just discussed, the Catechism stands squarely within the Catholic tradition, especially as it was formulated by Augustine and Thomas Aquinas. In this tradition the relationship between the Torah and the proclamation of Jesus is never seen dialectically; God in the Law does not appear *sub contrario*, as it were, in opposition to himself.[1] In tradition, it was never a case of dialectics, but rather of analogy, development in inner correspondence following the felicitous phrase of Saint Augustine: "The New Testament lies hidden in the Old; the Old is made explicit in the New." In regard to

[1] Those who heard this talk understood this sentence as a reference to Luther's view of the relation between the two Testaments. In fact I was thinking of particular aspects of Luther's thought, but of course I was also aware that it is impossible to do justice to a many-layered and nuanced work, such as that of the German Reformer, in a single sentence. It is not a question therefore here of judging or far less condemning Luther's theology of the Testaments. I am simply pointing out different models for dealing with the problem and will then go on to demonstrate the line of argument from Augustine to Thomas, which is the line adopted by the Catechism.

The numbers in parentheses refer (if not otherwise noted) to the numeration of the sections of the 1992 *Catechism of the Catholic Church.*

The following abbreviations, in addition to the usual abbreviations for the books of the Bible, are used here: CR = *Catechismus Romanus.*

NA = *Nostra aetate*, the declaration of the Second Vatican Council on the relationship between the Church and the non-Christian religions.

ST = Thomas Aquinas, *Summa Theologiae.*

the interrelation of both Testaments, the Catechism cites a significant text of Saint Thomas: "There were . . . , under the regimen of the Old Covenant, people who possessed the charity and grace of the Holy Spirit and longed above all for the spiritual and eternal promises by which they were associated in the New Law. Conversely, there exist carnal men under the New Covenant" (CCC 1964; ST I–II, 107, 1 ad 2).

The Torah as something integral

The above also means that the Law is read prophetically, in the inner tension of the promise. What such a dynamic-prophetic reading means appears in the Catechism first in twofold form: the Law is led to its fullness through the renewal of the heart (1968); externally this results in the suspension of ritual and juridical observances (1972). But here, needless to say, a new question arises. How could this happen? How is this compatible with fulfillment of the Law to the last iota? For, to be sure, one cannot simply separate out universally valid moral principles and transitory ritual and legal norms without destroying the Torah itself, which is something integral, which owes its existence to God's address to Israel. The idea that, on the one hand, there are pure morals that are reasonable and universal and,

---

Articulus stantis et cadentis Ecclesiae = a matter by which the Church stands or falls; *ex auctoritate divina* = by divine authority.

on the other, that there are rites that are conditioned by time and ultimately dispensable mistakes entirely the inner structure of the five books of Moses. The Decalogue as the core of the work of the Law shows clearly enough that the worship of God is completely inseparable from morals, cult, and ethos.

Jesus lives entirely under the Law of Israel— as mediator of the universality of God

However, we stand here before a paradox. The faith of Israel was directed to universality. Since it is devoted to the one God of all men, it also bore within itself the promise to become the faith of all nations. But the Law, in which it was expressed, was particular, quite concretely directed to Israel and its history; it could not be universalized in this form. In the intersection of these paradoxes stands Jesus of Nazareth, who himself as a Jew lived entirely under the Law of Israel but knew himself to be at the same time the mediator of the universality of God. This mediation could not take place through political calculation or philosophical interpretation. In both of these cases man would have put himself over God's Word and re-formed it according to his own standards.

Jesus did not act as a liberal reformer recommending and presenting a more understanding interpretation of the Law. In Jesus' exchange with the Jewish authorities of his time, we are not dealing with a confrontation between a liberal reformer and an ossified traditionalist hierarchy. Such a view, though common, fundamentally misunderstands the conflict of the New Testament and does justice neither to Jesus nor to Israel.

Rather Jesus opened up the Law quite theologically conscious of, and claiming to be, acting as Son, with the authority of God himself, in innermost unity with God the Father. Only God himself could fundamentally reinterpret the Law and manifest that its broadening transformation and conservation is its actually intended meaning. Jesus' interpretation of the Law makes sense only if it is interpretation with divine authority, if God interprets himself.

The quarrel between Jesus and the Jewish authorities of his time is finally not a matter of this or that particular infringement of the Law but rather of Jesus' claim to act *ex auctoritate divina*, indeed, to be this *auctoritas* himself. "I and the Father are one" (Jn 10:30).

The conflict that ended on the Cross

Only when one penetrates to this point can he also see the tragic depth of the conflict. On the one hand, Jesus broadened the Law, wanted to open it up, not as a liberal reformer, not out of a lesser loyalty to the Law, but in strictest obedience to its fulfillment, out of his being one with the Father in whom alone Law and promise are one and in whom Israel could become blessing and salvation for the nations. On the other hand, Israel "had to" see here something much more serious than a violation of this or that commandment, namely, the injuring of that basic obedience, of the actual core of its revelation and faith: Hear, O Israel, your God is one God.

Here obedience clashes with obedience, leading to the conflict that had to end on the Cross. Reconciliation and separation appear thus to be tied up in a virtually insolvable paradox.

In the Catechism's theology of the New Testament, the Cross cannot simply be viewed as an accident that actually could have been avoided or as the sin of Israel with which Israel becomes eternally stained in contrast to the pagans, for whom the Cross signifies redemption. In the New Testament there are not two effects of the Cross: a damning one and a saving one, but only a single effect, which is saving and reconciling.

Christian hope as the continuation
of the hope of Abraham

In this regard, there is an important text of the Catechism that interprets Christian hope as the continuation of the hope of Abraham and links it to the sacrifice of Israel: Christian hope has "its origin and model in the *hope of Abraham*, who was blessed abundantly by the promise of God fulfilled in Isaac, and who was purified by the test of the sacrifice" (1819). Through his readiness to sacrifice his son, Abraham becomes the

father of many, a blessing for all nations of the earth
(cf. Gen 22).

The New Testament sees the death of Christ in this
perspective, as a fulfillment of this course of events.
That means then that all cultic ordinances of the Old
Testament are seen to be taken up into his death and
brought to their deepest meaning. All sacrifices are acts
of representation, which, from symbols, in this great
act of real representation become reality, so that the
symbols can be dropped without one iota being lost.
The universalizing of the Torah by Jesus, as the New
Testament understands it, is not the extraction of some
universal moral prescriptions from the living whole of
God's revelation. It preserves the unity of cult and
ethos. The ethos remains grounded and anchored in
the cult, in the worship of God, in such a way that
the entire cult is bound together in the Cross, indeed,
for the first time has become fully real. According to
Christian faith, on the Cross Jesus opens up and fulfills the wholeness of the Law and gives it thus to the
pagans, who can now accept it as their own in this its
wholeness, thereby becoming children of Abraham.

4. The Cross

The historic and theological judgment about the responsibility of Jews and pagans for the Cross derives
in the Catechism from this understanding of Jesus, his
claim and fate.

No collective Jewish guilt

There is first the historical question of the course of the trial and execution. The headings of the four sections in the Catechism that treat this matter already show the direction: "Divisions among the Jewish authorities concerning Jesus"; "Jews are not collectively responsible for Jesus' death". The Catechism recalls that esteemed Jewish personages were followers of Jesus according to the witness of the Gospels, that, according to John, shortly before Jesus' death "many even of the authorities believed in him" (Jn 12:42). The Catechism also refers to the fact that on the day after Pentecost, according to the report of the Acts of the Apostles: "a great many of the priests were obedient to the faith" (Acts 6:7). James is also mentioned, who commented "how many thousands there are among the Jews of those who have believed; they are all zealous for the Law" (Acts 21:20). Thus it is elucidated that the report of Jesus' trial cannot substantiate a charge of collective Jewish guilt. The Second Vatican Council is expressly cited: "[N]either all Jews indiscriminately at that time, nor Jews today, can be charged with the crimes committed during his Passion. . . . [T]he Jews should not be spoken of as rejected or accursed as if this followed from holy Scripture" (597; NA 4).

"All sinners were the authors of Christ's Passion"

It is clear from what we have just now considered that such historical analyses—as important as they are—still do not touch the actual core of the question, since, indeed, the death of Jesus according to the faith of the New Testament is not merely a fact of external history but is rather a theological event. The first heading in the theological analysis of the Cross is accordingly: "Jesus handed over according to the definite plan of God"; the text itself begins with the sentence: "Jesus' violent death was not the result of chance in an unfortunate coincidence of circumstances, but is part of the mystery of God's plan" (599).

Corresponding to this, the part of the Catechism that explores the question of responsibility for Christ's death closes with a section entitled: "All sinners were the authors of Christ's Passion." The Catechism was able here to refer back to the Roman Catechism of 1566. There it states:

> If one asks why the Son of God accepted the most bitter suffering, he will find that besides the inherited guilt of the first parents it was particularly the vices and sins which men have committed from the beginning of the world up until this day and will commit from this day on till the end of time. . . . This guilt applies above all to those who continue to relapse into sin. Since our sins made the Lord Christ suffer the torment of the Cross, those who plunge themselves into disorders and crimes "crucify the Son of God on their own account and hold him up to contempt" (Heb 6:6).

The Roman Catechism of 1566, which the new Catechism quotes, then adds that the Jews, according to the testimony of the Apostle Paul "would not have

crucified the Lord of glory'' had they recognized him
(1 Cor 2:8). It continues: ''We, however, profess to
know him. And when we deny him by our deeds, we
in some way seem to lay violent hands on him'' (CR
I, 5, 11; CCC 598).

The drama of human sin and divine love

For the believing Christian who sees in the Cross, not
a historical accident, but a real theological occurrence,
these statements are not mere edifying commonplaces
in terms of which one must refer to the historical real-
ities. Rather these affirmations penetrate into the core
of the matter. This core consists in the drama of human
sin and divine love; human sin leads to God's love for
man assuming the figure of the Cross. Thus, on the one
hand, sin is responsible for the Cross, but on the other,
the Cross is the overcoming of sin through God's more
powerful love.

For this reason, beyond all questions of responsibility, the passage of the Letter to the Hebrews (12:24)
has the last and most important word to say on this subject, namely, that the blood of Jesus speaks another—a
better and stronger—language than the blood of Abel,
than the blood of all those killed unjustly in the world.
It does not cry for punishment but is itself atonement,
reconciliation.

Even as a child—even though I naturally knew nothing of all the things the Catechism summarizes—I

could not understand how some people wanted to de-
rive a condemnation of Jews from the death of Jesus
because the following thought had penetrated my soul
as something profoundly consoling: Jesus' blood raises
no calls for retaliation but calls all to reconciliation. It
has itself become, as the Letter to the Hebrews shows,
a permanent Day of Atonement to God.

A glance at the common mission of Jews and Christians in relation to the world

With the foregoing remarks we have only touched
upon the issues involved. In the light of the Catechism,
we have pondered the relationship between Jesus and
Israel and the Church's faith in Christ and its connection with the faith of Israel. In approaching this vast
topic, we restricted ourselves to one or two fundamental elements that the Catechism proposes as guidelines
for catechetical instruction in the Catholic Church.
While the foundations are thus laid for an examination of the question of Israel and the Church, it would
be impossible to examine them in detail here; such
work would also go beyond the limits of the teaching found in the Catechism. It is even less possible, in
the present compass, to tackle the large question of the
common mission of Jews and Christians in the modern
world. But I think, the basic task has nevertheless become clearer without my having to do this. Jews and
Christians should accept each other in profound inner

reconciliation, neither in disregard of their faith nor in denying it, but out of the depth of faith itself. In their mutual reconciliation they should become a force for peace in and for the world. Through their witness to the one God, who cannot be adored apart from the unity of love of God and neighbor, they should open the door into the world for this God so that his will may be done and so that it may become on earth "as it is in heaven": so that "his kingdom come".

II

THE NEW COVENANT

On the Theology of the
Covenant in the New Testament

*1. Testament or Covenant? From an Analysis
of the Word to the Subject at Issue*

We call the slim volume that forms the basis of the
Christian faith the "New Testament". However, this
book constantly refers back to another book, to which
it refers simply as "Scripture" or "the Scriptures", that
is, the Bible; this Bible grew throughout the history of
the Jewish people right up to the time of Christ, and
Christians call it the "Old Testament". So the totality
of the Scriptures on which the Christian faith rests is
God's "Testament" to mankind, issued in two stages,
as a proclamation of his will to the world.

This text was produced for a series of lectures by the Academy of
Moral and Political Sciences, Paris, on the theme "Contract, Pact,
and Covenant". A. Chouraqui presented the concept of covenant in
the Old Testament; my task was to present the New Testament counterpart. It was first published in *Internationale Katholische Zeitschrift
Communio* 24 (1995): 193–208.

The word "testament" was not imposed on the Scriptures: it is found in the Scriptures themselves. The title that Christians give to each book is not only meant to sum up the essential meaning of the book; it also brings to light the central theme of Scripture itself, thus giving a key to the whole of it. This very word "testament" is, in a way, an attempt to utter the "essence of Christianity" in a single, summary, expression —which is itself drawn from this fundamental source.

Agreement or ordinance?

But is the Latin word *testamentum* a good choice? Does it translate the basic meaning of the Hebrew and Greek text properly, or does it lead us on a false trail? We can see the translator's problem in the contrast between the old Latin version and that used by St. Jerome. The old Latin version says *testamentum*, but Jerome opted for *foedus* or *pactum*.[1] The term "testament" won out as a title for the book, but when considering what it contains, we follow Jerome and speak of the New and Old "Covenants", both in theology and in the liturgy.

Which is correct? Scholars have come to no agreement regarding the etymology of the Hebrew word *b^{e}rith*; the meaning intended by the biblical authors can only be gathered from the particular biblical contexts. One important pointer for an understanding of

[1] M. Weinfeld, "Berît", in: G. Botterweck and H. Ringgren, eds., *Theologisches Wörterbuch zum Alten Testament*, 1:781–808 (here 785).

the word is the fact that the Greek translators of the Hebrew Bible translate 267 of the 287 instances of the word *bᵉrith* by the Greek διαθήκη; that is, they did not use the words σπονδή or συνθήκη, which would be the Greek equivalent of "pact" or "covenant".[2] Evidently, their theological insight into the text led them to the view that the biblical content was not that of a *syn-theke*—a reciprocal agreement—but a *dia-theke*: it is not a case of two wills agreeing together but of *one* will establishing an ordinance.

God's free ordinance

Exegetical scholarship today is convinced, as far as I can see, that the men of the Septuagint were correct in understanding the biblical text in this way.[3] In the Bible, what we call "covenant" is not a symmetrical relationship between two partners who make a contractual agreement involving reciprocal obligations and penalties: this idea of a partnership among equals cannot be reconciled with the biblical concept of God. According to the latter, man is in no position to create a relationship with God, let alone give him anything and receive something in return; it is quite out of the question that man should bind God to obligations in

[2] Ibid.

[3] This becomes clear in M. Weinfeld's article (ibid.). Also see G. Quell and J. Behm, Διαθήκη, in G. Kittel, *Theologisches Wörterbuch zum Neuen Testament*, 2:105–37.

return for undertakings on his own part. If there is to be a relationship between God and man, it can only come about through God's free ordinance, in which his sovereignty remains intact.

The relationship is therefore completely asymmetrical, because God, for the creature, is and remains the "wholly Other". The "covenant" is not a two-sided contract but a gift, a creative act of God's love. This last statement, it is true, goes beyond the philological issue. Although the covenant is patterned on Hittite and Assyrian contracts between states, in which the lord imposes his law on his vassal, God's covenant with Israel is far more: here God, the King, receives nothing from man; but in giving him his law, he gives him the path of life.

The contractual act of a love story

This raises a question. Formally, the Old Testament type of covenant corresponds strictly to the genre of the vassal contract with its asymmetrical structure. But its concept of God has a dynamism that transforms from within the whole essence of the event, the whole meaning of this sovereign ordinance. If it is seen no longer in terms of a contract between states but in the image of bridal love (as in the Prophets, most movingly in Ezekiel 16), if the contractual act is presented as a love story between God and the Chosen People, what happens to the inherent asymmetry? True, even marriage in the ancient Near East is not a matter of partnership but is seen in patriarchal terms from the point of view of the man, the master. But the Prophets' portrayal of God's passionate love goes beyond what is to hand in the purely legal forms of the Orient. On the one hand, given God's infinite "Otherness", the concept of God must seem to be the most radical heightening of the asymmetry; and, on the other hand, the true nature of *this* God must seem to create a two-sidedness that is totally unexpected.

What is the difference between the "Old" and the "New Covenant"?

At this point it is necessary to take a preliminary look at the philosophical treatment that the theme of "covenant" has received in the history of Christian theology. If covenant is an image that originally comes from the sphere of law, what corresponds to it in the sphere of philosophy is the category of *relatio*. In the ancient world, from an entirely different starting point and with an almost opposite significance, it was clear that the *relatio* between God and man could only be asymmetrical. Greek philosophy deduced, on the basis of the logic inherent in metaphysical thinking, that the immutable God could not enter into mutable relationships and that relationship is proper to mutable man. In the relationship between God and man, therefore, one could speak only of a *relatio non mutua*, a relatedness without reciprocity: man refers to God, but God does not refer to man. The logic seems unavoidable. Infinity requires immutability, and immutability excludes relationships that come and go in time and as a result of time.

But does not the message of the covenant say the very opposite? Before going into the questions arising from this analysis of the meaning of *b^erith* and *diatheke*, we must address the most important New Testament texts on the subject of covenant. They present us with a further question: What is the difference between the "Old" and the "New Covenant"? What constitutes the unity of the concept of covenant in the two Testaments, and in what way does it differ between them?

It is impossible, of course, to examine the whole span of New Testament covenant theology in the present article. I would like simply to shed some light, by way of example, on a number of central passages in the Pauline Letters and on the idea of covenant in the texts concerning the Last Supper.

2. Covenant and Covenants in the Apostle Paul

What strikes us first of all is that Paul makes a firm disjunction between the covenant in Christ and the Mosaic covenant; this is how we usually understand the difference between the "Old" and the "New" Covenant. Paul's sharpest contrast between the two

Testaments is to be found in 2 Corinthians 3:4–18 and Galatians 4:21–31. Whereas the term "New Covenant" comes from prophecy (Jer 31:31) and so forms a link between both parts of the Bible, the expression "Old Covenant" occurs only in 2 Corinthians 3:14. By contrast, the Letter to the Hebrews speaks of the "first covenant" (9:15) and calls the New Covenant —in addition to this classic term—the "aeonic" or "eternal" Covenant (13:20), an expression adopted in the "words of institution" of the Roman Canon of the Mass, where it speaks of the "new and everlasting Covenant".

The covenant in Christ and the Mosaic covenant

In 2 Corinthians, Paul sets these two in diametrical opposition: the former is transitory; the latter abides perpetually. Transience is a characteristic of the Mosaic covenant; Paul sees this symbolized by the stone Tables of the Law. Stone signifies what is dead; anyone who remains exclusively in the realm of the Law written in stone remains in the realm of death.

Here Paul was no doubt thinking of Jeremiah's promise that, in the New Covenant, the Law would be engraved on the people's hearts; also he may have been thinking of Ezekiel, who had said that the heart of stone would be replaced by a heart of flesh.[4]

---

[4] Cf. R. Bultmann, *Der zweite Brief an die Korinther* (Göttingen, 1976), 76.

While the text initially stresses most strongly the fact that the Mosaic covenant is now a thing of the past, doomed to collapse, a new and altered perspective emerges at the end: Anyone who turns to the Lord will find that the veil is taken away from his heart, and he will see the Law's inner radiance, its pneumatic light; so he will be able to read it correctly.

The multiplicity of images used by Paul here, as so often, somewhat obscures his meaning; but, at all events, the image of the removal of the veil indicates a modification of the idea of the Law's transitory nature: when the veil is removed from the heart, what is substantial and ultimate about the Law comes into focus. Thus the Law itself becomes Spirit, identical with the new order of life in the Spirit.

The covenant with Noah, with Abraham, and with Jacob-Israel

The strict antithesis between the two Covenants, the Old and the New, that Paul develops in 2 Corinthians 3 has fundamentally marked Christian thought ever since, whereas the subtle interplay between "the letter" and "the spirit"—expressed in the image of the "veil" —has been hardly noticed. Most importantly, it has largely been forgotten that other Pauline texts portray the drama of God's history with men in a much more nuanced way.

In chapter 9 of Romans, Paul sings the praises of Israel: among God's gifts to his people are "the covenants", and according to the Wisdom tradition they are a plurality.[5] Indeed, the Old Testament speaks of three signs of the covenant: the sabbath, the rainbow, and circumcision; these correspond to three stages of the covenant, or three covenants. The Old Testament relates the covenant with Noah, with Abraham, with Jacob-Israel, the Sinai covenant, and God's covenant with David.

Each of these covenants has its specific nature, and we shall have to return to them. Paul is well aware that, prior to the Christian history of salvation, the word "covenant" had to be understood and spoken of in the plural; out of these various covenants he selects two particularly, sets them up in mutual opposition, and refers each one to the covenant in Christ: these are the covenant with Abraham and the covenant with Moses. He sees the covenant made with Abraham as the real, fundamental, and abiding covenant; according to Paul, the covenant made with Moses was interposed (Rom 5:20) 430 years after the Abrahamic covenant (Gal 3:17); it could not abrogate the covenant with Abraham but constituted only an intermediary stage in God's providential plan.

Legal prescription and promise

God's pedagogy with mankind operates in such a way that its individual props are jettisoned when the goal

---

[5] Rom 9:4. Cf. H. Schlier, *Der Römerbrief* (1977), 287.

of the educational process is reached. Particular paths are abandoned, but the meaning remains. The covenant with Moses is incorporated into the covenant with Abraham, and the Law becomes a mediator of promise. Thus Paul distinguishes very sharply between two kinds of covenant that we find in the Old Testament itself: the covenant that consists of legal prescriptions and the covenant that is essentially a promise, the gift of friendship, bestowed without conditions.[6]

In the Pentateuch, in fact, the word *b^erith* is often equivalent to "law" and "commandment". A *b^erith* is something that is commanded; the Sinai covenant in Exodus 24 appears essentially as "the imposition of laws and obligations on the people".[7] This kind of covenant can also be broken; Israel's history in the Old Testament continually appears to be a history of the broken covenant.

A unity in tension: The one Covenant in the plurality of covenants

By contrast, the covenant with the Patriarchs is regarded as eternally in force. Whereas the covenant imposing obligations is patterned on the vassal contract, the covenant of promise has the royal grant as its model.[8] To that extent Paul, with his distinction

[6] Weinfeld, "Berît", 799f.
[7] Ibid., 784.
[8] Ibid., 799.

between the covenant with Abraham and the covenant with Moses, has rightly interpreted the biblical text. This distinction, however, also supersedes the strict opposites of the Old and the New Covenant and implies that all history is a unity in tension: the one Covenant is realized in the plurality of covenants.

If this is so, there can be no question of setting the Old and the New Testaments against each other as two different religions; there is only *one* will of God for men, only *one* historical activity of God with and for men, though this activity employs interventions that are diverse and even in part contradictory—yet in truth they belong together.

3. The Idea of the Covenant in the Texts of the Last Supper

The interrelatedness of the many covenants and the one Covenant brings us to the heart of our topic. We have to tread with particular care here, because we are dealing with deeply rooted Jewish and Christian habits of thought, which must be illuminated—and in part corrected—through recourse to the original biblical message.

The accounts of the Last Supper are decisive for a correct understanding of the New Testament concept of covenant. They constitute, so to speak, the New Testament counterpart to the account of the Sinai covenant (Ex 24), and thus they provide the foundation for the Christian conviction about the New Covenant in Christ. Here we do not need to enter into the complicated exegetical discussions regarding the relationship between text and event and the genesis of the texts and their chronological relationship (these issues remain matters of dispute): our aim is simply to examine what the texts say, just as they are, in response to our questions.

The new unity of covenant ideas

What is not disputed is that the four "institution" accounts (Mt 26:26–29; Mk 14:22–25; Lk 22:17–20; I Cor 11:23–26), on the basis of their textual form and the theology it manifests, can be divided into two groups: the Markan-Matthean tradition and what we find in Paul and Luke. The main difference between them lies in the word referring to the cup. In Matthew and Mark the words uttered over the chalice are: "This is my blood of the covenant, which is poured out for many." Matthew adds, "for the forgiveness of sins". In Paul and Luke, however, the cup is referred to in these words: "This cup is the new covenant in my blood"; and Luke adds, "which is shed for you". "Covenant" and "blood" stand here in grammatical apposition. In Matthew-Mark the gift of the cup is "the blood", which is further defined as "the blood of the covenant".

In Paul-Luke the cup is "the new covenant", which is described as ratified "in my blood".

A second difference is that only Luke and Paul speak about the *new* covenant. A third important difference is that only Matthew and Mark give us the words "for many". Both strands of tradition base themselves on Old Testament covenant traditions, but each strand selects a different reference point. In this way all the essential covenant ideas flow together in the ensemble of utterances at the Last Supper and are fused into a new unity.

The Sinai covenant heightened
to a staggering realism

What traditions are we talking about? The reference to the cup in Matthew and Mark comes straight from the account of the making of the Sinai covenant. Moses sprinkles the sacrificial blood first on the altar, which represents the hidden God, and then on the people, saying, "Behold the blood of the covenant which the Lord has made with you in accordance with all these words" (Ex 24:8). Here very ancient concepts are taken up and elevated to a higher plane.

The scholar G. Quell has defined the archaic idea of the covenant as it appears in the stories of the Patriarchs: "To make a covenant means both to form a blood association with an alien and to include this alien covenant-partner in one's own community, thus entering into juridical fellowship with him." The fictitious blood relationship thus created "makes the participants brothers of the same flesh and blood". "The covenant creates a whole, which is peace"[9]—Shalom.

The Sinai blood ritual means that God does with these people, on their way through the desert, what until then only particular tribal associations had done; namely, he enters into a mysterious blood relationship with them, in such a way that he now belongs to them and they to him. True, the content of the relationship established here, between God and man (in itself a paradox), is defined by the word publicly declared, the "book of the covenant". It is by appropriating this word, by the life that comes from it and with it, that the relationship—represented cultically in the ritual of the blood—comes into being.

When Jesus offers the cup to the disciples and says, "This is the blood of the covenant", the words of Sinai are heightened to a staggering realism, and at the same time we begin to see a totally unsuspected depth in them. What takes place here is both spiritualization *and* the greatest possible realism. For the sacramental blood fellowship that now becomes a possibility brings those who accept it into an utterly concrete—and corporeal —community with this incarnate human being, Jesus, and hence with his divine mystery.

[9] Quell and Behm, Διαθήκη, 115f.

A new relationship with God

Paul described this new "blood relationship" with God, which comes about through fellowship with Christ, in a bold and shocking metaphor: "Do you not know that he who joins himself to a prostitute becomes one body with her? For, as it is written, 'The two shall become one' (Gen 2:24). But he who is united to the Lord becomes *one* pneuma (one spirit) with him" (1 Cor 6:17). These words present us with an entirely different kind of relationship: a sacramental relationship with Christ —and hence with God—detaches man from his own material and transitory world and lifts him up into the being of God, to which the Apostle gives the word pneuma. The God who has come down thus draws man up into his own new realm. Being related to God means a new and profoundly transformed level of existence for man.

But how can what is specific to Jesus be communicated to men? We have seen that, in the Sinai covenant, it is through acceptance of the word, acceptance of God's legal code, that people are incorporated into his mode of being. The Last Supper texts do not speak of this directly. Instead, what we have is the word that recalls Isaiah 53, the Song of the Suffering Servant: ". . . which is shed for many". In this way the prophetic tradition is linked to, and interprets, the Sinai tradition. Jesus takes others' destiny into his own; he lives for them, and he dies for them.

Covenant renewal in its highest possible form

At this point we can confidently follow the Church Fathers in going beyond what is directly found in the text, without losing its fundamental sense. Christ's death only brings the fulfillment of what was begun in the Incarnation. The Son has taken humanity into himself and now brings it home to God: "Sacrifices and offerings thou hast not desired, but a body hast thou prepared for me. . . . Lo, I have come . . ." (Heb 10:5–7; Ps 40:7–9). It is because the Son has handed himself over to God that his "blood" is now given to men as the blood of the covenant. Body has become word, and word has become body in the act of love that is the specifically divine mode of being; from now on, through participation in the sacrament, it is to become man's mode of being.

With regard to the issue of the nature of the covenant, it is important to note that the Last Supper sees itself as making a covenant: it is the prolongation of the Sinai covenant, which is not abrogated, but renewed. Here renewal of the covenant, which from earliest times was doubtless an essential element in Israel's liturgy[10], attains its highest form possible. In this perspective we should see the Last Supper as one further renewal of

---

[10] Mowinckel, in his search for the *Sitz-im-Leben* and origin of the Sinai covenant, even put forward the thesis that it reflected an annual celebration including a theophany and the proclamation of the Law; cf. Weinfeld, "Berît", 793f.

the covenant, but one in which what heretofore was performed ritually is now given a depth and density—by the sovereign power of Jesus—which could not possibly have been envisaged. This may also enable us to understand that both the Letter to the Hebrews and the Gospel of John (in Jesus' high-priestly prayer) go beyond the traditional link between the Last Supper and the Pasch and see the Eucharist in connection with the Day of Atonement; the institution of the Eucharist is to be seen as a cosmic Day of Atonement—an idea also suggested in Saint Paul's Letter to the Romans (3:24f.).[11]

The New Covenant established by God is itself present in the faith of Israel

Before proceeding, we must take a brief look at the Lukan-Pauline tradition of the word over the cup. As we saw, what the cup contains is "the new covenant in my blood". This is an unmistakable reference to the prophetic tradition we find in Jeremiah 31:31–34, which begins with the words, "They broke my covenant" (31:32). God, according to the Prophet, will replace the broken Sinai covenant with a New Covenant

---

[11] The connection between John 17 and the liturgy of Yom Kippur is convincingly brought out by A. Feuillet, *Le Sacerdoce du Christ et ses ministres* (Paris, 1972), esp. 39–63. Cf. also H. Gese, "Die Sühne" in: H. Gese, *Zur biblischen Theologie* (Munich, 1977), 85–106 (here especially 105f.).

that cannot be broken: this is because it will not confront man in the form of a book or a stone tablet but will be inscribed on his heart. The conditional covenant, which depended on man's faithful observance of the Law, is replaced by the unconditional covenant in which God binds himself irrevocably.

We are unmistakably here in the same conceptual milieu as we found earlier in 2 Corinthians, with its contrast between the two covenants. However, the Last Supper words make it clearer than 2 Corinthians that it is not simply a question of the opposition of the Old and New Testaments as two separate worlds; rather, both ideas, that of the broken covenant and that of the other, new covenant established by God, featured in the faith of Israel.

Admonished by the Prophets, and as a result of the suspension of the Temple cult during the Exile and the recurring trials that followed it, Israel well knew that it had broken the covenant more than once. The broken tablets at the foot of Mount Sinai were the first, dramatic expression of the broken covenant. And when the restored tablets were lost forever after the Exile, it was all the more evident that that fateful hour had resulted in a permanent condition. Israel also knew that the constantly repeated celebration of the renewal of the covenant could not restore the tablets, for only God could give them and fill them with his handwriting. It also knew, however, that God had not withdrawn his love for Israel; it knew that God himself renewed his covenant and that the promise of the New Covenant was not merely in the future: because of God's unfailing love, the covenant was already present in the promise.[12]

Covenant renewal is not superfluous in the New Covenant

Conversely, Christians must be aware that the definitive nature of the unbreakable New Covenant, present to them in the flesh and blood of the Risen Christ, does not mean that their infractions of this Covenant are insignificant. Covenant renewal has not become superfluous in the New Covenant; in fact, it is characteristic of it. The command to repeat the words of the Last Supper, which are an expression of the making of the Covenant, means that the New Covenant is continually confronting man in its newness. It remains ever new and is always one and the same Covenant.[13]

---

[12] Cf. E. Zenger, ed., *Der Neue Bund im Alten: Zur Bundestheologie der beiden Testamente*, QD 146 (Freiburg, 1993), esp. the articles by C. Dohmen, "Der Sinaibund als Neuer Bund nach Ex 19–34", 51–83, and A. Schenker, "Der nie aufgehobene Bund", 85–112; E. Zenger, *Das Erste Testament: Die jüdische Bibel und die Christen*, 4th ed. (Düsseldorf, 1994); also the review by H. Seebaß and the reply by E. Zenger in: *Theologische Revue* 90 (1994): 265–78. In his *Der Römerbrief* (Freiburg, 1977), 340, H. Schlier puts it well: "The radiant hope of eschatological salvation and homecoming . . . rests on everyone who is an Ἰσραηλίτης."

[13] It seems to me that this is what is meant when Hebrews 3:13 applies to Christians the "today" of Psalm 95 and its warning against that hardness of heart which can lead to loss of the "land of rest".

Two central questions

Having endeavored to establish the New Testament idea of covenant from the Pauline covenant theology and the words of the Last Supper, we must sum up our results and decide what answers to give to the two central questions that arose in our examination of these texts:

How are the individual covenants related to each other, and, in particular, how is the New Covenant related to the covenants we find in Israel's Bible?

What is the ultimate relationship between testament and covenant? Should we speak of a one-sided or two-sided covenant?

4. *The One Covenant and the Many Covenants*

Christian tradition generally, on the basis of Pauline theology and the eucharistic words of the Last Supper, has thought in terms of two covenants, the New and the Old. This picture of two alternatives is characterized by a series of antitheses. The Old Covenant is particular and concerns the "fleshly" descendants of Abraham. The New Covenant is universal and is addressed to all peoples. Thus the Old Covenant depends on the principle of inheritance, and the New Covenant on a spiritual relationship created by sacrament and faith. The Old Covenant is conditional: since it depends on the keeping of the Law, that is, on man's behavior; it can be broken and has been broken. Since its essential content is the Law, it is expressed in the formulation, "If you do all this. . . ." This "if" draws man's changeable will into the very essence of the covenant itself and thus makes it a provisional covenant.

The irrevocable gift of friendship

By contrast, the covenant sealed in the Last Supper, in its inner essence, seems "new" in the sense of the prophetic promise: it is not a contract with conditions but the gift of friendship, irrevocably bestowed. Instead of law we have grace. The rediscovery of Pauline theology at the Reformation laid special emphasis on this point: not works, but faith; not man's achievement, but the free bestowal of God's goodness. It emphatically underlined, therefore, that what was involved was not a "covenant" but a "testament", a pure decision and act on God's part.[14] This is the context in which we must understand the teaching that it is God alone who does everything. (All the *solus* terms—*solus Deus, solus Christus*—must be understood in this context.)

[14] This is very clear in the article in ThWNT by G. Quell and J. Behm; cf. also the article "Bund", by Hempel, Goppelt, Jacob, and Wiesner in: RGG I (1957): 1512–23.

What conclusions can we draw from all this? It seems to me that we have become aware of two facts that complement the one-sidedness of these antitheses and make visible the inner unity of the history of God's relations with man, as it is portrayed in the whole Bible, Old and New Testaments together.

The inner continuity of salvation history

First of all we must remember that the fundamentally "new" covenant—the covenant with Abraham—has a universalist orientation and looks toward the many sons who will be given to Abraham. Paul was absolutely right: the covenant with Abraham unites in itself both elements, namely, the intention of universality and the free gift. To that extent, right from the beginning, the promise to Abraham guarantees salvation history's inner continuity from the Patriarchs of Israel down to Christ and to the Church of Jews and Gentiles.

With regard to the Sinai covenant, we must again draw a distinction. It is strictly limited to the people of Israel; it gives this nation a legal and cultic order (the two are inseparable) that as such cannot simply be extended to all nations. Since this juridical order is constitutive of the Sinai covenant, the law's "if" is part of its essence. To that extent it is conditional, that is, temporal; within God's providential rule it is a stage that has its own allotted period of time.

Paul set this forth very clearly, and no Christian can

revoke it; history itself confirms this view. But this does not mean that there is nothing more to be said about the covenant with Moses and "Israel according to the flesh". For the Law is not only a burden imposed on believers—as we are inclined to think, due to one-sided emphasis of the Pauline antitheses. As seen by Old Testament believers, the Law itself is the concrete form of grace. For to know God's will is grace. And to know God's will is to know oneself, to understand the world, to know what our destination is. It means that we are liberated from the darkness of our endless questioning, that the light has come, that light without which we can neither see nor move. "You have not shown your will to any other nation": for Israel, at least for its best representatives, the Law is the visibility of the truth, the visibility of God's countenance, and so it gives us the possibility of right living. Are not these our questions: Who am I? Where am I going? What shall I do to put my life in order? The hymn to God's word that we find—in ever-new variations—in Psalm 119 expresses this joy of being delivered, the joy of knowing God's will. For his will is our truth and therefore our way; it is what all men are looking for.

Jesus the Messiah; the Torah of the Messiah

This can help us to understand what Paul means when, in Galatians 6:2, in line with the Jewish messianic hope, he speaks of the Torah of the Messiah, the Torah of

Christ. Paul's view, too, is that the Messiah, the Christ, does not make man lawless, does not deprive him of justice. Rather, it is characteristic of the Messiah—he who is "greater than Moses"—that he brings the definitive interpretation of the Torah, in which the Torah is itself renewed, because now its true essence appears in all its purity and its character as grace becomes undistorted reality. In his commentary on the Letter to the Galatians, Heinrich Schlier says, "The Torah of Jesus the Messiah is in fact an 'interpretation' of the Mosaic Law, . . . an 'interpretation' on the basis of the Cross of Jesus the Messiah." His plenary power "manifests the Law, in its essential meaning, as the creative, life-giving message of the One who has fulfilled it."[15]

The Torah of the Messiah is the Messiah, Jesus, himself. It is to him that the command, "Listen to him", refers. In this way the "Law" becomes universal; it is grace, constituting a people which becomes such by hearing the word and undergoing conversion. In this Torah, which is Jesus himself, the abiding essence of what was inscribed on the stone tablets at Sinai is now written in living flesh, namely, the twofold command of love. This is set forth in Philippians 2:5 as "the mind of Christ". To imitate him, to follow him in discipleship, is therefore to keep the Torah, which has been fulfilled in him once and for all.

Thus the Sinai covenant is indeed superseded. But

---

[15] H. Schlier, *Der Brief an die Galater* (Göttingen, 1962), 273.

once what was provisional in it has been swept away, we see what is truly definitive in it. So the expectation of the New Covenant, which becomes clearer and clearer as the history of Israel unfolds, does not conflict with the Sinai covenant; rather, it fulfills the dynamic expectation found in that very covenant. From the perspective of Jesus, the "Law and the Prophets" are not in opposition: Moses himself—as Deuteronomy tells us—is a prophet and can only be understood correctly if he is read as such.

5. "Testament" and Covenant

The question of whether what we are dealing with is a covenant or a testament, a two-sided interaction or a one-sided action, is closely bound to the question of the difference between the covenant in Christ and the covenant with Moses. The basic structure of all the covenants we find in the Old and New Testaments is asymmetrical, that is, it expresses a sovereign action, not a contract between two equal partners. The *law* is an action by which the king binds his vassals and makes them such; *grace* is an action that is freely given without any preceding merit.

God binds himself to partnership

This idea, that the testament is one-sided, no doubt corresponds to the idea of God's greatness and sovereignty;

it is also determined, of course, by a particular social structure. The rulers of the ancient Orient always act one-sidedly, in a sovereign manner: no one can be on the same level as they are. But even this sociological context, with its asymmetrical order, is torn up and jettisoned in the Bible; thus our picture of God also acquires a new form. God acts, certainly; yet, practically from the outset, he binds himself, as it were, so that what comes into being is something like a partnership.

Augustine put this aspect very beautifully: "God is faithful, for he has put himself under a debt to us, not as if he had received anything from us, but by promising us so much. The word of promise was too little for him: he wanted to bind himself in writing, by giving us, as it were, a handwritten version of his promises."[16] If we read the Prophets, we find that this is not perceived as a merely external, positive act: Israel's faith recognizes, in this act of binding himself, God's very nature. Thus it differs from the picture of God that one would expect in the context of an Eastern ruler. "When Israel was young, I loved him", God says, in the Prophet Hosea, of his manner of binding himself to his people. It follows that, even when the covenant is continually being broken, God, by his very nature, *cannot* allow it to fall. "How could I abandon you, Ephraim; how could I give you up, Israel? . . . My heart turns against me, my compassion flames forth" (Hos 11:1, 8).

What is presented here as a brief sketch is devel-

---

[16] *En in ps* 109, 1 CChr 40:1601.

oped into a great story of futile love—or, rather, indestructible and hence ultimately not futile love—in Ezekiel 16.

The entire drama of broken faith on the part of the people ends with this pronouncement: "Then you shall remember and be ashamed; for shame you shall no more dare to open your mouth, because I have forgiven all that you have done" (Ezek 16:63).

Binding himself even as far as the Cross

All these texts presuppose the mysterious account of the making of the covenant with Abraham, in which the Patriarch, in oriental fashion, divides the sacrificial animals into two parts. As a rule, the covenant partners pass between the divided animal halves, thereby invoking a conditional curse upon themselves: let it be to me as to these animals if I break the covenant. Abraham has a vision of a smoking oven and a blazing torch—images of theophany—passing between the animal parts. God seals the covenant by guaranteeing his faithfulness in an unmistakable symbol of death. Is it possible, then, for God to die? Can he punish himself?

Christian interpretation was bound to see in this text a mysterious and previously indecipherable image of the Cross, in which God, through his Son's death, guarantees that the covenant cannot be broken; thus he hands himself over to mankind in a radical way (Gen 15:1–21).

It belongs to God's nature to love what he has created; so it belongs to his nature to bind himself and, in doing so, to go all the way to the Cross. Thus, as the Bible sees it, the unconditional nature of God's action results in a genuine two-sidedness: the testament becomes a covenant. The Church Fathers described this novel two-sidedness, which arises from faith in Christ as the Fulfiller of the promises, as the "incarnation of God" and the "divinization of man". God binds himself by giving Scripture as the binding word of promise, but he goes beyond this by binding himself, in his own existence, to the human creature by assuming human nature. Conversely, this means that man's primal dream comes true, and man becomes "like God": in this exchange of natures, which gives us the fundamental theme of Christology, the unconditional nature of the divine covenant has become a definitively two-sided relationship.

6. The Picture of God and Man in the Idea of Covenant

Thus we see that Christology is a synthesis of New Testament covenant theology, which always rests on the unity of the entire Bible. Of necessity, however, this christological concentration leads us beyond a mere interpretation of biblical texts; we are faced with the question of the nature of man and God; it becomes necessary to exert ourselves to reach a rational understanding. This means that theology must look for a philosophy that is acceptable to it. It is not my task here to say what that might be. I would only return, briefly, to the philosophical category we have already met, corresponding to the theme of the covenant, namely, *relatio*. For in asking about the covenant, we are asking whether there can be a relationship between God and man, and what kind of relationship it might be.

The God of the Bible is a God-in-relationship

We observed that, in the ancient world, man could orient himself to God through knowledge and love but that any notion of a relationship between the eternal God and temporal man was regarded as absurd and hence impossible. The philosophical monotheism of the ancient world opened up a path for biblical faith in God and its religious monotheism, which seemed to facilitate once again the lost harmony between reason and religion. The Fathers, who started from the assumption of this harmony between philosophy and biblical revelation, realized that the one God of the Bible could be affirmed, in his identity, through two predicates: creation and revelation, creation and redemption. But these are both relational terms. Thus the God of the Bible is a God-in-relationship; and to that extent, in the essence of his identity, he is opposed to the self-enclosed God of philosophy.

This is not the place to trace the complicated intellec-

tual struggle that sought to establish the interrelatedness
of reason and religion. It had followed from the idea of
God's unique oneness, yet now it was practically called
into question once again. In the context of the present
topic, all I will say is that, as a result of this struggle, a
new philosophical category—the concept of "person"
—was fashioned, a concept that has become for us the
fundamental concept of the analogy between God and
man, the very center of philosophical thought.[17]

Covenant as God's self-revelation, "the radiance of his countenance"

The meaning of an already existing category, that of
"relation", was fundamentally changed. In the Aris-
totelian table of categories, relation belongs to the
group of accidents that point to substance and are dependent on it; in God, therefore, there are no accidents.
Through the Christian doctrine of the Trinity, *relatio*
moves out of the substance-accident framework. Now
God himself is described as a trinitarian set of relations,
as *relatio subsistens*.[18] When we say that man is the im-

---

[17] This is beautifully clear in C. Schönborn, *Die Christus-Ikone* (1984),
esp. 30–54 (English trans.: *God's Human Face: The Christ-Icon* [San
Francisco, 1994], 14–33).

[18] Even if the entire scope of the process is not yet clear, we can see
the refashioning of the inherited categories in Augustine, *De Trin.* 5,
5, 6 (PL 42, 914): "Quamobrem nihil in eo (= in Deo) per accidens
dicitur, quia nihil ei accidit; nec tamen omne quod dicitur, secundum
substantiam dicitur . . . hoc non secundum substantiam dicuntur, sed

age of God, it means that he is a being designed for relationship; it means that, in and through all his relationships, he seeks that relation which is the ground of his existence. In this context, covenant would be the response to man's imaging of God; it would show us who we are and who God is. And for God, since he is entirely relationship, covenant would not be something external in history, apart from his being, but the manifestation of his self, the "radiance of his countenance".

---

secundum relativum; quod tamen relativum non est accidens, quia non est mutabile." ("Wherefore nothing in Him is said in respect to accident, since nothing is accidental to Him, and yet all that is said is not said according to substance . . . they [the Father and the Son] are so called, not according to substance, but according to relation, which relation, however, is not accident, because it is not changeable.")

III

THE NEW MANNA

Homily for the 19th Sunday
in Year B, 1997

Texts for the Liturgy:
First Reading: 1 Kings 19:4–8
Second Reading: Ephesians 4:30–5:2
Gospel: John 6:41–51

Our first reading, from the First Book of Kings, brings us to one of the crucial junctures in Israel's history. In the Northern Kingdom of the ten tribes that had separated themselves from Judah, belief in God of the fathers, belief in the one God, had practically vanished into the sand. This resulted from the rule of a heathen queen and the king who followed her wishes. Elijah stood alone, the only remaining Prophet of this God, over against four hundred prophets of the fertility cult of the god Baal.

This homily was preached on August 10, 1997, at a service for the Catholic Integrated Community in Wolfesing near Munich.

Fire from heaven

In this situation, when the task of presenting the message of God seems to have become hopeless, Elijah calls to heaven and is heard. Fire comes down from heaven, and the four hundred prophets are killed by the sword. Very soon, however, Elijah has to realize that this is not the way in which God triumphs; he realizes that faith cannot be established by such signs, by force. The heathen queen retains her power, and at a deeper level it is plain that the human heart is inclined to heathenism and estranged from the unknown God; it likes to settle down with the things of this world and its habits. If there is to be faith once again, other things must happen, different things.

Elijah has to flee before the king's might. Now even the last Prophet of Yahweh has vanished from the land. God seems to have collapsed; his history is about to end. Elijah, too, is resigned: he has lost. His own great heart is broken, he wants to die; it is hopeless, everything is futile.

The flame of Horeb

It is at this moment, when he lets go of his own greatness, when he no longer believes that he himself is able to reestablish God's kingdom, that God's new paths begin to open up. Now God himself can act, must act. Elijah's flight becomes a journey of faith.

Elijah has to go back, for forty days and forty nights, to the place where the story of faith actually began,

Mount Horeb. For now it becomes clear that the real disaster is the fact that the flame of Horeb, the flame of the knowledge of God, of his word, of the justice that flows from it, of a right ordering of life, of the worship of God, has gone out. Israel may now be living in its own land, but in reality it has gone back to Egypt; it has become heathen again, ready for exile; it has lost itself.

If this land is to be really *the land*, if the promise is to be fulfilled, something else is necessary, something that creates true community of life, namely, the presence of God's word, a readiness to listen to him, a life lived in relation to him. Elijah must go back, he must recapitulate Israel's history—the forty years are concentrated into the forty days and nights—and make a pilgrimage to Horeb on behalf of Israel.

This kind of return, this continually new appropriation of history, needs to happen again and again. It happens in Jesus' forty days in the wilderness. The Church does it in the forty days of the preparation for Easter: we endeavor to get away from the heathenism that weighs us down, that is always driving us away from God, and we set off toward him once again. So, too, at the beginning of the Eucharist, in the confession of sin, we are always trying to take up this path again, to set out, to go to the mountain of God's word and God's presence.

The God who is "poor"

Elijah arrives at God's mountain of Horeb; the revelation takes place again, and he is brought into a new phase. For now he sees that the One whom he had sought in the fire is not in the storm and not in the wielding of force. God is in the quiet, gentle breath of the Holy Spirit. He sees that God is different, other: he is quiet compared to the noise of this world.

So Elijah's experience brings us directly to the New Testament, to the Gospel and to the figure of Jesus, in whom what is said about the Servant of God is fulfilled: *He will not cry aloud in the streets; he will not break a bruised reed or quench a smoldering wick.* In him, finally, that God appears of whom Elijah was granted a foretaste on Horeb. This God is not loud; he cannot compete with the powers of this world. He is the "poor" God, the God whose only weapons are the humble weapons of love and truth, and who therefore always seems to be the loser. Nonetheless he is the only true, saving power in this world.

I think we should stop here for a while. We too experience God's powerlessness, we too seem to see him as the One who always comes off worst. We would prefer him to be stronger, more tangible, more powerful in the face of all this world's failures, dangers, and menaces. We too must learn once more, as it were, this mystery of Horeb that has taken shape in Christ; we must learn that it is only in the silent, barely noticeable things that what is great takes place, that man becomes God's image and the world once more becomes the radiance of God's glory.

Let us ask the Lord to give us a receptivity to his gentle presence; let us ask him to help us not to be so deafened and desensitized by this world's loud outcry that our receptivity fails to register him. Let us ask him that we may hear his quiet voice, go with him, and be of service together with him and in his way, so that his kingdom may become present in this world.

The new manna

We can discern something else in this story of Elijah, something that links up directly with today's Gospel. Not only is there a repetition of Israel's forty years in the desert: there is also a repetition of the story of the manna, albeit now in a very simple form. Here there is no water springing from the rock, no manna raining down from heaven: for Elijah there is simply a piece of bread and a jug of water; he is to take it as food for the forty days. This is the new manna, now in a humble and simple form.

The real meaning of the story of the manna, then, is not that it comes down from heaven like rain, or that it is of this or that shape or composition, or that it appears on the ground in a certain form: what is essential about the manna is how it was interpreted even in the Old Testament: *that he might make you know that man*

does not live by bread alone, but that man lives by everything
that proceeds out of the mouth of the Lord.

The manna was to show that man can live only in
dependence on God. Man is to learn to live by God,
for then he really lives, then he has eternal life, for God
is eternal. Anyone who lives with him and in dependence on him is already in that real life which reaches
out beyond death. Living in dependence on God means
not being one's own master, not wanting to take charge
of the world oneself; it means saying good-bye to the
dream of autonomy and of being one's own boss, rec-
ognizing that we cannot do it on our own and learning
to accept our life day by day from his hands, without
anxiety and full of confidence.

God has become our bread

In today's Gospel this core meaning of the manna
(what, we might say, it actually *is*), namely, that we
are to live in dependence on God, not on ourselves,
becomes utterly concrete. We can live by God because
God now lives for us. We can live by God because he
has made himself one of us, because he himself, as it
were, has become our bread. We can live by God because he gives himself to us, not only as the Word, but
as the Body that is given up for us and is given to us,
ever new, in the sacrament.

What this "living by God" means is stressed in the
Gospel in two sentences that belong together: *Everyone*

who believes in the Son has eternal life. The bread which I shall give for the life of the world is my flesh. Living by God means first of all believing, it means being in touch with him, entering into an inner harmony with him.

However, since God himself has become body, since he has come among us, has become one of us (and has not ceased to be one of us, for, of course, he is risen), this "believing" no longer means a kind of reaching out in thought, in questioning, in hope and prayer, toward some great, infinite mystery. Now, belief has itself become incarnate. Believing means living by the God whose Body is in the Church; it means being nourished by this embodied God who encounters us in the sacraments and who has ultimately become so incarnate that in the Eucharist he gives himself to us as Body, so that we can enter into his life: just as he lives for us, so we live by him and for him.

"Be imitators of God!"

The second reading tells us the same thing in a different way, and in very daring words: *Be imitators of God!* That seems extravagant language. How could we human beings be expected to imitate God? Yet the desire to do this is deep within us. The people who want to have everything, who cannot have enough money, the people who finally manage to get everything, do everything, who want to live life for themselves, who want just to be themselves—they all think they are living like God: everything is there for my benefit; I am not there for anyone else's benefit.

But in reality, while they think they have really become gods, their life is a caricature of God: it is pitiful, empty, and hopeless.

There is a still higher way of trying to imitate God. We find it in the case of Prometheus, and even in Elijah: by bringing down fire from heaven. Today's equivalent of this is technology: we bring the power of creation down to our level so that we can manipulate it; we give ourselves sovereign authority over this world, and so we live as masters of the world, holding it in our hands and no longer needing God.

But even this more sophisticated and ambitious way of attempting to imitate God is doomed to failure. For it tortures both the world and us.

Be imitators of God! Again, this does not happen in a loud or imposing manner.

Be imitators of God! This takes place in the quiet way which is God's, for that is the way his divinity lives. Paul translates it simply: *Love one another.* That is to imitate God, the trinitarian God.

The miracle of the manna made concrete

Lest we should find this too meaningless, Paul makes it concrete for us, just as concrete as God himself has made it: *Walk in love, as Christ loved us and gave himself up for us, a fragrant offering and sacrifice to God.* We imitate God, we live by God, like God, by entering into Christ's manner of life. He has climbed down from his divine being and become one of us; he has given himself and does so continually.

Finally, Paul makes God's "littleness", his "quietness"—which is, after all, the true divinity—even more concrete, so that it does not remain entrapped in the lofty speculation that cannot speak to our ordinary life.

Paul lists the ways in which we live as God does: *Let all bitterness and wrath and anger and clamor and slander be put away from you, with all malice, and be kind to one another, tenderhearted, forgiving one another, as God in Christ forgave you.*

It is by these little daily virtues, again and again, that we step out of our bitterness, our anger toward others, our refusal to accept the other's otherness; by them, again and again, we open up to each other in forgiveness. This "littleness" is the concrete form of our being like Christ and living like God, imitating God; this is how the miracle of the manna is made concrete. He has given himself to us so that we can give ourselves to him and to one another.

Now we celebrate the Eucharist: the Lord gives himself to us as the true manna. Let us ask him that we may not only do this ritually and liturgically but be inwardly touched by him. Let us ask that the holy light of Sinai, which has become concretely close in him, shall shine in us, transform us, and so enable us to become like God, to become proper human beings.

Amen.

IV

THE DIALOGUE OF THE RELIGIONS AND THE RELATIONSHIP BETWEEN JUDAISM AND CHRISTIANITY

Immediately after the conquest of Constantinople by the Turks in 1453, Cardinal Nicholas Cusanus wrote a remarkable book, entitled *De pace fidei*. The collapsing empire was shattered by religious disputes; the Cardinal himself had taken part in the ultimately failed attempt to unite the Eastern and Western Church; and now Islam had once again come within the horizon of Western Christendom.

It was Cusanus' experience, through the events of his time, that religious peace and secular peace were closely connected. He tried to answer this issue by putting forward a kind of utopia—intended, however, as an utterly concrete service to peace: "Christ, the

---

This text was produced for a session of the Academy of Moral and Political Sciences, Paris. Rabbi Sztejnberg, who had suggested the topic, presented the Jewish perspective. This helps to account for the broad span of the topic, its concrete emphases, and the limitations of its execution. It first appeared in: *Internationale Katholische Zeitschrift Communio* 26 (1997): 419‒29.

world's Judge, seeing that the evil of multiple religions on earth is becoming intolerable, summons a heavenly council",[1] in which "seventeen representatives of the various nations and religions are shown, by the divine Logos, how the religious concerns of all can be settled in the Church represented by Peter."[2]

In all the teachings of wisdom, Christ says here, "you do not find a different faith in each one; rather, they each presuppose one and the same faith." "God as Creator is the Triune and the One; as the Infinite he is neither Triune nor One, nor anything that can be uttered. For the names that are attributed to God come from creatures, whereas he in himself is ineffable, sublime above everything that can be named and uttered."[3]

1. From Christian Oikumene *to the Dialogue of Religions*

In the meantime this projected "heavenly council" has come down to earth and, since the voice of the Logos can be heard only in a fragmentary way, it has inevitably become more complicated. The ecumenical movement had gradually come into being in the

---

[1] H. U. von Balthasar, *Glaubhaft ist nur Liebe* (Einsiedeln, 1963), 10 (English trans.: *Love Alone: The Way of Revelation* [London, 1968]).

[2] R. Haubst, "Nikolaus v. Kues", in: LThK, 2d ed., 7:988−91, this quotation 990.

[3] *De pace fidei* 7, 11, 16, 10, 62 (*Op. omnia*, vol. 7 [Meiner, 1959]), quoted by Balthasar, *Glaubhaft*, 10f.

nineteenth century, initially as a result of the missionary experience of the Protestant churches: they found
that the multiplicity of their splintered denominations
was putting a substantial obstacle in their way as they
sought to witness to the pagan world. They saw church
unity as an indispensable condition of mission. Ecumenism, in this sense, was first and foremost a phe-
nomenon of world Protestantism, an outward thrust
proceeding from the inner world of Christianity.[4]
If the universal claim of its message is to be put
forward, those who bear it must not contradict one
another; they must not come as representatives of
splinter groups, exhibiting distinctive features and antagonisms that are rooted solely in the history of the
Western world. Subsequently the impulse of the ecumenical movement spread more and more to the whole
of Christendom. Eastern Orthodoxy was the first to
join it, albeit in the beginning with cautious provi-
sos. The Catholic Church's approach to the ecumenical movement began with individual groups in coun-
tries that suffered in a special way from the Church's
divisions, until the Second Vatican Council flung the
Church's doors open to the search for the unity of all
Christians.

Initially, as we saw, the encounter with the non-
Christian world served only as a trigger for the search

[4] Cf. R. Rouse and S. C. Neill, *A History of the Ecumenical Movement, 1517–1948* (London, 1954); H. J. Urban and H. Wagner, eds.
Handbuch der Ökumenik, vol. 2 (Paderborn, 1986).

for Christian unity. But it was inevitable that Christians would begin to take notice of the actual religious message of the world religions. After all, the gospel was not being proclaimed to religion-less people who had no knowledge of God. It was no longer possible to overlook the fact that Christians were addressing a world deeply penetrated by religious convictions and stamped by these convictions even in the tiniest details of daily life, so that the religiosity of these people put to shame the somewhat tired faith of Christians. It was less and less sufficient, therefore, to describe the adherents of other religions simply as pagans, or purely negatively as "non-Christians". It was necessary to get to know what made them what they were; one had also to ask whether it was right simply to destroy their religious world, or whether it was perhaps possible, or even an obligation, to understand them from within and bring into Christianity the inheritance that was theirs.

In this way Christian ecumenism gradually expanded into the dialogue of religions.[5] Of course, this dialogue is not meant simply to recapitulate the path taken by the "history of religions" scholarship of the nineteenth and early twentieth centuries. This scholarship was based on a liberal-rationalistic standpoint, supposedly above and beyond the religions, and thought it could

[5] Cf. K. Reiser, *Ökumene im Übergang: Paradigmenwechsel in der ökumenischen Bewegung?* (Munich, 1989).

evaluate the individual religions with the assurance of enlightened reason. Nowadays the dominant conviction is that there can be no such standpoint; that religion, if it is to be understood, must be experienced from within. Only on the basis of this experience, which is necessarily individual and time-bound in its origin, can there be mutual understanding and thus a deepening and purification of religion.

2. The Question of Unity in Diversity

Once we have become cautious about making definitive evaluations, the question of unity in diversity becomes a pressing one. The ecumenical problem of the religions emerges today against the background of a world that, on the one hand, is getting closer and closer together and becoming a single common arena of human history and, on the other hand, is shaken by wars, torn by growing tensions between rich and poor, and, finally, threatened in its very foundations by the misuse of our technological mastery over the earth. On the basis of this threefold threat, a new canon of ethical values has formed and is attempting to define mankind's essential moral task, in this its historic hour, in terms of the three concepts of peace, justice, and preservation of creation. Religion and morality are not identical, yet they are indissolubly connected.

Now, therefore, at a time when mankind has acquired the ability to destroy itself and its planet, it is clear that the religions share a common responsibility to overcome this temptation. They are being tested in a special way against this canon of values, which is seen more and more as their joint challenge and, hence, as a basis for their unification. Hans Küng uttered what many were thinking when he said, "No world peace without peace between the religions"; in these words he declared that peace between the religions, ecumenism across the religions, is a duty imposed on all religious communities.[6]

But how can this be done? How is genuine encounter possible, given the diversity of religions and the antagonisms that, even today, are always breaking out in violent forms? What kind of unity can there be? On what basis can one even begin to look for this unity? If we make the effort to grasp the relationships that exist within the confusing plurality of the world religions, it is possible to draw a preliminary distinction between tribal religions and universal religions; although, it must be said, even the tribal religions reveal underlying common patterns that, in turn, are related to the great impulses of the universal religions.

To that extent there is a certain to-and-fro between both provinces; we cannot go into it any deeper here, but it does give us the right, in considering ecumenism

---

[6] On the problems associated with the "world ethos" postulated by Küng in this connection, cf. R. Spaemann, "Weltethos als 'Projekt'", *Merkur: Deutsche Zeitschrift für europäisches Denken*, no. 570/571, 893–904.

across the religions, to concentrate our attention primarily on the universal religions. According to the present state of scholarship, there seem to be two fundamental types of universal religion, which J. A. Cuttat describes in terms of "interiority and transcendence".[7] At the risk of oversimplifying things, I would like to contrast them—on the basis of what is most concrete in them and of what constitutes the central act of their piety—as the theistic and the mystical types of religion. If this diagnosis is correct, we are presented with two ways of conducting ecumenism across the religions: either we can try to incorporate the theistic religion into the mystical type, which means that we regard the mystical type as the larger, more all-embracing, in which the theistic heritage can find its place; or we try to take the opposite path.

Today a third alternative has appeared on the scene. I call it the pragmatic solution: all religions should give up the endless dispute about truth and recognize that their true essence, what they are all aiming at, is found in orthopraxy; in turn, the path of orthopraxy seems to be clearly outlined by the challenges of the present day. Orthopraxy, ultimately, can only exist in the service we

---

[7] J. A. Cuttat, "Expérience chrétienne et spiritualité orientale" in: *La Mystique et les mystiques* (Paris, 1965); J. A. Cuttat, *Begegnung der Religionen* (Einsiedeln, 1956). On this whole issue of the dialogue of religions, cf. H. Bürkle, *Der Mensch auf der Suche nach Gott—die Frage der Religionen*, Amateca, vol. 3 (Paderborn, 1996). Also useful is O. Lacombe, *L'Élan spirituel de l'hindouisme* (Paris, 1986).

give to peace, justice, and the protection of creation.
The religions could all keep their formulas, forms, and
ritual, but everything should be geared to this *right prac-
tice*: "By their fruits you shall know them." They could
all retain their customs and usages; all dispute would be
superfluous, and yet they would be one in whatever the
hour were to demand of them.

3. The Greatness and Limits
of the Mystical Religions

In what follows I would like briefly to examine these
three possible ways; and when it comes to the theistic way, given the demands of the present hour, I
shall reflect in particular on the relationship between
Christian and Jewish monotheism, leaving aside, for
reasons of brevity, the problem of the third great figure in monotheistic religion—Islam. At a time when
we have learned to doubt even whether we can know
the transcendent at all, and when we are extremely un-
easy about the potential for intolerance when claims
of truth are made in this area, it seems that the future must belong only to mystical religion. It alone
seems to have taken the proscription of images with
complete seriousness; Panikkar, for instance, says that
Israel's religion must be regarded as iconolatry even
though it forbids images, since it insists on a personal,
named God.[8]

[8] R. Panikkar, *La Trinidad y la experiencia religiosa* (Barcelona, 1989):

Religion no longer defined by its positive content

Here, by contrast, in the context of a strongly apophatic theology, no claims are made as to knowledge of the divine. Religion is no longer defined by its positive content or by institutional or sacral features. It is now found entirely at the level of mystical experience, which means that all conflict with scientific reason is excluded from the outset. "New Age" is, so to speak, the proclamation of the age of mystical religion. Its brand of rationality refuses to claim knowledge; in its own way, therefore, it is tolerant, while allowing man that unfettering of his being that he needs if he is to live and endure finitude.

The divine, personal or non-personal

If this were to be the right path, ecumenism would have to see itself as promoting universal understanding by withdrawing all positive propositions (which means those claiming to be composed of truth) and dismantling sacral structures in favor of the merely functional. What is being called for here is not simply the total surrender of previously existing theistic forms: there seems to be a growing consensus that both ways of seeing the divine should be regarded as compatible: that ultimately they are saying the same thing. Ultimately

---

German edition: *Trinität: Über das Zentrum menschlicher Erfahrung* (Munich, 1993), 35–43.

it does not matter whether the divine is conceived in personal or non-personal terms. The God who speaks and the silent depth of being are, it is suggested, only two different ways of conceiving the ineffable that lies beyond all concepts. Israel's central imperative, "Hear, O Israel, your God is a living God", which remains a constitutive element for both Christianity and Islam, loses its contours. Whether one prostrates oneself before the God who speaks or lets oneself sink into the silent depth of being is ultimately a matter of indifference. The worship that the God of Israel demands and the emptying of consciousness that forgets its own "I" and is dissolved in the Infinite can ultimately be seen as variants of one and the same attitude vis-à-vis the Infinite.

The cosmos no longer
has anything to do with God

This seems to yield the best possible solution. The existing forms can exist, but the relativity of all external forms must be acknowledged. We must realize that we are united in the search for the depth of being in an inwardness that leaves even our own "I" behind, enabling us to receive the gift of consoling contact with the Ineffable, enabling us to emerge, strengthened, into the everyday world.

Doubtless things are being said here that can contribute to a deepening of the theistic religions. The latter, in fact, have never been without the mystical current and apophatic theology.[9] It was always taught that everything uttered is ultimately only a distant reflection of the Ineffable and that the dissimilarity to what we can imagine and think is always greater than any similarity.[10] To that extent, worship is always involved with interiorization, and interiorization with self-transcendence. Yet the identification of both paths and their ultimate withdrawal does not lead to fulfillment in the mystical path. For in that case, the empirical world drops out of all relationship with the divine. The concept of creation is no longer applicable. The cosmos, which is no longer creation, has nothing to do with God.

Salvation lies outside the world

The same applies to history. God no longer reaches into the world; it is literally god-less and empty of God. Religion can no longer create any community of thought and will; it becomes, as it were, individual therapy. Salvation lies outside the world; we are given no instructions on how to act in it: all we have is the strength we

[9] Cf. L. Bouyer, *Mysterion: Du mystère à la mystique* (Paris, 1986) (English trans.: *The Christian Mystery: From Pagan Myth to Christian Mysticism* [Edinburgh, 1990]).

[10] For example, the Fourth Lateran Council, 1215: "Quia inter creatorem et creaturam non potest similitudo notari, quin inter eos maior sit dissimilitudo notanda" ["between Creator and creature no similitude can be expressed without implying an even greater dissimilitude"] (DS 806).

may acquire through regular withdrawal into the spiritual dimension. But the latter has, as such, no definable message for us. We are left to ourselves in our worldly affairs.

Today those who are trying to work out a new version of ethics often take this as their starting point, and even moral theology has begun to come to terms with this approach. In such a case, however, ethics becomes something that we have constructed. It ceases to be binding and, more or less hesitantly, obeys our own interests.

Faith in God cannot dispense with a truth whose substance can be articulated

At this point we can see, perhaps, that the theistic model, while it has more in common with the mystical model than one might think, is not reducible to it. For an essential part of our faith in the one God is the acknowledgment of God's will. Worship of God is not only a sinking into him: it also gives us back to ourselves, it challenges us in the midst of our everyday lives, summoning all the powers of our mind, feeling, and will. However important the apophatic element may be, faith in God cannot dispense with truth, with a truth whose substance can be articulated.

4. The Pragmatic Model

Then what about the pragmatic model we have already mentioned: Is this not a solution that is applicable both to the demands of the modern world and to the concrete reality of the religions?

A short circuit

It does not take much reflection to see that what we have here is a short circuit. Of course our efforts on behalf of peace, justice, and the protection of creation are of the highest importance, and religion should doubtlessly provide a vehicle for substantial action in this regard. But the religions have no a priori knowledge of what serves peace here and now, or of how social justice can be built within and between states, or of how creation can best be protected and cultivated out of a sense of responsibility to the Creator. All these things must be worked out rationally and on an individual basis.

This always requires free debate between differing opinions and respect for different paths. Often this pluralism of paths cannot be resolved, and if the wearying rational debate is cut short by a religiously motivated moralism that declares one path to be the only right one, religion is perverted into an ideological dictatorship, with a totalitarian passion that does not build peace but destroys it. Religion cannot be forced into the service of practical-political objectives; the latter would become an idol; man, making God the slave of his plans, would degrade both God and himself.

Lucifer's most subtle temptation

More than forty years ago, J. A. Cuttat wisely wrote: "To try to make mankind better and happier by bringing the religions together is one thing. To pray ardently for the unification of all mankind in the love of the same God is something else. And it may be that the former is Lucifer's most subtle temptation, designed to frustrate the latter."[11]

This refusal to turn religion into political moralism does not mean, of course, that education for peace, justice, and love for the Creator and creation are not part and parcel of the task of the Christian faith and of every religion: here too we are right to say, "By their fruits you shall know them."

5. Judaism and Christianity

Now let us turn to the theistic path and its possibilities in the "council of religions". As we know, theism manifests itself in history in the three great forms of Judaism, Christianity, and Islam. First of all, therefore,

---

[11] *Begegnung der Religionen*, 84.

we must explore the possibility of reconciling the three great monotheisms with one another, prior to bringing them into dialogue with the mystical path. As already indicated, I restrict myself here to the first split in the monotheistic world, that between Judaism and Christianity; overcoming this split is fundamental to the relationship of both of them to Islam. Obviously, my remarks can only be a modest suggestion concerning this vast problem. I would like to put forward two ideas.

Through Jesus the God of Israel has become the God of all the nations of the world

The average man may be impressed by a formula such as this: "The Hebrew Bible, the 'Old Testament', links Jews and Christians; faith in Jesus Christ as the Son of God and Redeemer divides them." It is easy to see, however, that this comparison between what links together and what separates is superficial. The first thing to be said is that it is through Christ that Israel's Bible has come to non-Jews and has become their Bible too.

When the Letter to the Ephesians says that Christ has broken down the wall separating the Jews from the other religions of the world and has created unity, this is not empty theological rhetoric but an empirical state of affairs, even if the empirical realm does not exhaust the full theological meaning. For, through the encounter with Jesus of Nazareth, the God of Israel has become the God of the nations of the world. Through him the promise has indeed been fulfilled that the nations shall pray to the God of Israel as the one God, that the "mountain of the Lord" will be lifted up above the other mountains.

Jesus: God's Son and Servant

Israel may find it impossible to see Jesus as the Son of God as Christians do; but it is not impossible for them to see him as the Servant of God who carries the light of his God to the nations. Conversely, even if Christians look for the day when Israel will recognize Christ as the Son of God and the rift that separates them will be healed, they should also acknowledge God's providence, which has obviously given Israel a particular mission in this "time of the Gentiles". The Fathers say that the Jews, to whom Holy Scripture was first entrusted, must remain alongside us as a witness to the world.

But what does this witness say? This brings us to my second argument. I think we can say that two things are essential to the faith of Israel.

Faith, hope, and love and the three dimensions of time

First of all there is the Torah, the commitment to God's will and the establishment of his rule, his kingdom in this world.

Secondly there is the hope, the expectation of the Messiah; the expectation, even the certainty, that God himself will step into this history and create justice— for the forms of justice we ourselves set up are very imperfect.

In this way the three dimensions of time are linked: obedience to the will of God is referred to a Word that has been uttered, which is now a datum of history and has to be realized anew in obedience. By this obedience, which makes part of God's justice present in time, we go forward into a future in which God will gather together all the fragments of time and incorporate them as a totality into his justice.

This fundamental structure has not been abandoned in Christianity. The threefold constellation of faith, hope, and love corresponds in some measure to the three dimensions of time: the obedience of faith accepts the Word that comes from eternity and is uttered in history, transforming it into love, in the present, and so opening the door of hope.

It is characteristic of Christian faith that all three dimensions are held together and lived through in the figure of Christ, who simultaneously takes them and extends them into eternity. In him, time and eternity co-inhere, and the infinite abyss between God and man is bridged. For Christ is the one who has come to us without ceasing to be with the Father; he is present in the believing community, and he is also the one who is yet to come.

The Church's messianic expectation

The Church, too, *waits for* the Messiah she already knows, the Messiah who has yet to manifest his glory. Obedience and promise are inextricably linked in the Christian faith. Christ, for the Christian, is Sinai present here and now, the living Torah, who imposes duties upon us and challenges us to obedience, at the same time drawing us into the broad arena of love and its inexhaustible possibilities. Thus he is the guarantor of our hope in the God who will not allow history to fall into the non-being of what is past, but holds it fast and brings it to its destination.

It follows, therefore, that the figure of Christ both links and separates Israel and the Church. It is not within our power to overcome this separation, but it keeps both of us to the path that leads to the One who comes. To that extent the relationship between us must not be one of enmity.

6. The Christian Faith and the Mystical Religions

So we come to the question we have so far deferred. What, in concrete terms, is Christianity's position in the dialogue of religions? Is theistic, dogmatic, and hierarchically ordered religion necessarily intolerant? Does belief in the truth formulated by dogma make us incapable of dialogue? Does readiness for peace imply the jettisoning of truth?

The mystical dimension of the Christian faith

I would like to answer this question in two stages. First we must once more remember that the Christian faith has within it a mystical and an apophatic side. One of the reasons why the modern encounter with the religions of Asia will be significant for Christians is that they will be reminded once again of this side of their faith; one-sided and hardened positions in statements of Christian faith are broken down.

An objection may be raised here: What about the doctrines of the Trinity and the Incarnation? Are they not radical forms of this hardened positivity, suggesting that God is formally graspable and can be held in concepts and that the mystery of God can be trapped in fixed forms and a historically datable figure?

At this point one should remember the dispute between Gregory of Nyssa and Eunomius: Eunomius had asserted that God was fully understandable on the basis of the given revelation, whereas Gregory opposed him by interpreting trinitarian theology and Christology as *mystical* theology, inviting us to an infinite journey to a God who is always infinitely greater.[12]

---

[12] Cf. F. Dünzl, *Braut und Bräutigam: Die Auslegung des Canticum durch Gregor von Nyssa* (Tübingen, 1993); Bouyer, *Mysterion*, 225ff.; of abiding value is H. U. von Balthasar, *Présence et pensée: Essai sur la philosophie religieuse de Grégoire de Nysse* (Paris, 1942) (English trans.: *Presence and Thought: An Essay on the Religious Philosophy of Gregory of Nyssa* [San Francisco, 1995]).

The cloud of mystery

In fact, trinitarian theology is apophatic insofar as it cancels the simple idea of the human person acquired from human experience; while it does acknowledge the God who speaks, the God-Logos, it simultaneously preserves the greater silence that comes from the Logos and bids us enter it.

Something similar can be said of the Incarnation. Yes, God becomes concrete, tangible in history. He approaches men in bodily form. But this very God, become graspable, is utterly mysterious. The humiliation he himself has chosen, his "kenosis", is in a new way, so to speak, the cloud of mystery in which he both conceals and reveals himself.[13] For what greater paradox could there be than this, that God is vulnerable and can be killed? The Word, which the Incarnate and Crucified One is, always far surpasses all human words; thus God's kenosis is the place where the religions can meet without claims of sovereignty.

Plato's Socrates, particularly in the *Apology* and *Crito*, points to the connection between truth and defenselessness, between truth and poverty. Socrates is credible because his commitment to "God" brings him neither position nor possessions; on the contrary, it consigns him to poverty and ultimately to the role of an accused

---

[13] Cf. B. Stubenrauch, *Dialogisches Dogma: Der christliche Auftrag zur interreligiösen Begegnung* (Freiburg, 1995), esp. 84–96.

criminal.[14] Poverty is the truly divine manifestation of truth: thus it can demand obedience without involving alienation.

7. Concluding Points

The question remains: What does this mean in concrete terms? What can be expected from Christianity, thus understood, in the dialogue of religions? Does the theistic, incarnational model bring us farther than the mystical and the pragmatic?

Let me speak plainly: Anyone who expects the dialogue between religions to result in their unification is bound for disappointment. This is hardly possible within our historical time, and perhaps it is not even desirable.

What then? I would like to say three things.

No renunciation of truth

First, the encounter of the religions is not possible by renouncing truth but only by a deeper entering into it. Scepticism does not unite people. Nor does mere pragmatism. Both only make way for ideologies that become all the more self-confident as a result.

The renunciation of truth and conviction does not elevate man but hands him over to the calculations of utility and robs him of his greatness.

[14] For example, *Apologia* 31c: "I believe I can produce a satisfactory witness for the truth of what I say, namely, my poverty." *Crito* 48c–d.

What we need, however, is respect for the beliefs of others and the readiness to look for the truth in what strikes us as strange or foreign; for such truth concerns us and can correct us and lead us farther along the path. What we need is the willingness to look behind the alien appearances and look for the deeper truth hidden there.

Furthermore, I need to be willing to allow my narrow understanding of truth to be broken down. I shall learn my own truth better if I understand the other person and allow myself to be moved along the road to the God who is ever greater, certain that I never hold the whole truth about God in my own hands but am always a learner, on pilgrimage toward it, on a path that has no end.

Criticism of one's own religion

Second, if this is the case, if I must always look for what is positive in the other's beliefs—and in this way he becomes a help to me in searching for the truth —the critical element can and may not be missing; in fact, it is needed. Religion contains the precious pearl of truth, so to speak, but it is always hiding it, and it is continually in danger of losing sight of its own essence. Religion can fall sick, it can become something destructive. It can and should lead us to truth, but it can also cut men off from truth. The criticism of religion found in the Old Testament is still very relevant today. We may find it relatively easy to criticize the religion of others, but we must be ready to accept criticism of ourselves and of our own religion.

Karl Barth distinguished in Christianity between religion and faith. He was wrong if he was intending to make a complete separation between them, seeing only faith as positive and religion as negative. Faith without religion is unreal; religion belongs to it, and Christian faith, of its very nature, must live as a religion. But he was right insofar as the religion of the Christian can succumb to sickness and become superstition: the concrete religion in which faith is lived out must continually be purified on the basis of truth, that truth which shows itself, on the one hand, in faith and, on the other hand, reveals itself anew through dialogue, allowing us to acknowledge its mystery and infinity.

Proclamation of the gospel as a dialogical process

Third: Does this mean that missionary activity should cease and be replaced by dialogue, where it is not a question of truth but of making one another better Christians, Jews, Moslems, Hindus, or Buddhists? My answer is No. For this would be nothing other than total lack of conviction; under the pretext of affirming one another in our best points, we would in fact be failing to take ourselves (or others) seriously; we would be finally renouncing truth. Rather, the answer must be that mission and dialogue should no longer be opposites but should mutually interpenetrate.[15]

Dialogue is not aimless conversation: it aims at conviction, at finding the truth; otherwise it is worthless. Conversely, missionary activity in the future cannot proceed as if it were simply a case of communicating to someone who has no knowledge at all of God what he has to believe.

There can be this kind of communication, of course, and perhaps it will become more widespread in certain places in a world that is becoming increasingly atheistic. But in the world of the religions we meet people who have heard of God through their religion and try to live in relationship with him.

In this way, proclamation of the gospel must be necessarily a dialogical process. We are not telling the other person something that is entirely unknown to him; rather, we are opening up the hidden depth of something with which, in his own religion, he is already in touch.

The reverse is also the case: the one who proclaims is not only the giver; he is also the receiver. In this sense,

---

[15] For a proper understanding of mission, cf. H. Bürkle, *Missionstheologie* (Stuttgart, 1979); P. Beyerhaus, *Er sandte sein Wort. Theologie der christlichen Mission*, vol. 1: *Die Bibel in der Mission* (Wuppertal, 1996). R. Spaemann makes important points in his contribution, "Ist eine nicht-missionarische Praxis universalistischer Religionen möglich?" in: *Theorie und Praxis: Festschrift N. Lobkowicz zum 65. Geburtstag* (Berlin, 1996), 41–48.

what Cusanus saw in his vision of the heavenly council, which he expressed as both a wish and a hope, should come true in the dialogue of religions: the dialogue of religions should become more and more a listening to the Logos, who is pointing out to us, in the midst of our separation and our contradictory affirmations, the unity we already share.